ALSO BY MICHAEL LEBOEUF

How to Win Customers and Keep Them for Life

Getting Results
(formerly published as
*The Greatest Management
Principle in the World*)

Working Smart

THE PERFECT BUSINESS

HOW TO MAKE A MILLION FROM HOME WITH
No Payroll
No Employee Headaches
No Debts
and No Sleepless Nights!

MICHAEL LeBOEUF

A FIRESIDE BOOK
Published by Simon & Schuster

FIRESIDE
Rockefeller Center
1230 Avenue of the Americas
New York, NY 10020

First Fireside Edition 1997

FIRESIDE and colophon are registered trademarks
of Simon & Schuster Inc.

Designed by Irving Perkins Associates, Inc.

Manufactured in the United States of America

1   3   5   7   9   10   8   6   4   2

The Library of Congress has cataloged the Simon & Schuster
edition as follows:
LeBoeuf, Michael.
The perfect business : how to make a million from home with no payroll, no employee headaches, no debts, and no sleepless nights /
Michael LeBoeuf.
p.   cm.
Includes index
1. Home-based businesses. 2. Home-based businesses—Management.
3. New business enterprises—Management. 4. Success in business.
I. Title
HD2333.L43   1996   96-6970
658'.041—dc20   CIP

ISBN 0-684-80272-4
0-684-83345-X (Pbk.)

ACKNOWLEDGMENTS

With special thanks to

Artie and Richard Pine for many years of loyalty, enthusiasm, friendship, and wise guidance of my writing career.

Fred Hills and Burton Beals for their editorial help and expertise.

Joe Vizzini, my accountant, who helped me title the book when he told me, "Michael, you've created the perfect business."

Neil Baum, Deanna Berg, Jimmy Caplan, Carolyn Long, Ed Rigsbee, Susan RoAne, Jeff and Marc Slutsky, Elke Stevens, Robert Tucker, and Barry Wishner for their ideas and encouragement.

To ELKE,
my best friend, my love, and the miracle of my life

CONTENTS

INTRODUCTION

Your Ticket to Freedom

> You are never given a dream without also being
> given the power to make it true. . . . You may have to
> work for it, however.
>
> —RICHARD BACH

Getting rich and becoming a millionaire is the pinnacle of the American dream. But for the overwhelming majority of Americans, it remains just that—a dream and nothing more. Worse yet, for many of us, getting rich is the farthest thing from our minds. Most of us are preoccupied with making enough money just to pay the bills.

Are you worried about being able to make a living and maintain your current lifestyle? Most of us are. It's no wonder when you consider that:

- *Corporate America is eliminating 3,000 jobs each day, and the overwhelming majority of them are gone forever.* That means that almost 3,000 people a day are being forced to find new ways to make a living, in addition to those already looking for work and those entering the labor force.
- *Americans are working longer and getting poorer.* The average American worker is working 160 hours a year more than he was at the end of the 1960s. That's the equivalent of

adding an extra month's work per year. Between 1984 and 1991 median net worth for U.S. households declined 15 percent, and the downward trend in net worth is continuing. Between 1989 and 1992 men aged 25 to 54 who left one full-time job for another saw their earnings decline an average of 20 percent. From 1989 to 1993 median household income declined for all income groups except those in the top 20 percent.

• *Only 1 out of every 20 Americans ever achieves financial independence.* The rest of us depend on our current earnings, the earnings of others, charity, or the government to survive for our entire lives.

Enough gloom and doom. I don't want to be mistaken for an economist. I want you to know that you can earn the freedom and wealth you want operating from the comfort of your home or anywhere you want. Is it easy? Hell, no. Does it take time, effort, and commitment? You bet. But it isn't nearly as difficult as most people imagine and it's getting easier with every passing year. Is it worth it? Yes, a millionfold.

Let me share some good news with you. We are living in a new era with incredible opportunities for getting rich. The information age is bringing millions of us more freedom and wealth than we ever imagined. Those who are doing well realize that success in this new era means doing many things differently than in the past. To capitalize on the new economy requires holding different assumptions, using different tools, and playing by a different set of rules. Unfortunately, too many of us are still trying to make a living with the assumptions, habits, and tools of a bygone era. And those are the same people who are working harder and getting poorer. Don't let this happen to you.

Although statistics report that most Americans are working harder and getting poorer, I'm happy to report that my experience is just the opposite. In 1977 I started a second career with a notepad and a ballpoint pen. I was a professor making about $20,000 a year, hoping to supplement my income by writing a book. With that decision, I began a second career in the business of creating and selling information. In 1991 my net worth reached $1 million and today it's closer to $2 million. If I continue to work, save, and invest, I know that some day my net worth will be $3 million, then $4 million, then $5 million, and so on. And if I lose it all tomorrow, I know I can attain millionaire status much faster and with less effort than it took the first time.

"So what?" you say. "The world is full of millionaires." You're right. Today there are literally millions of households in the United States with a net worth of at least a million dollars.

In today's world a million dollars isn't great wealth. Becoming a millionaire isn't going to land you a segment on "Lifestyles of the Rich and Famous." But it will buy you freedom from the stresses and strains of everyday life that plague at least 95 percent of the population. All those people aren't buying lottery tickets just for fun. While a million dollars isn't the wealth it once was, it's still a whole lot of money.

What's most important is *how* I achieved financial freedom. I started with no money, just my wits. I never borrowed a cent. I never took any stressful risks. I didn't quit my day job until I was well on my way to financial independence. I have never hired a single employee or rented office space. And no one who knows me has ever accused me of being a workaholic. Until I was 25 I thought manual labor was a Mexican diplomat.

But along the way, I learned the attitude and the mind-set for making good decisions. And that made all the difference. I'm convinced that almost anyone can achieve as much or more success as I have if he or she has enough desire and self-discipline and knows how to make the right decisions. And that's the most important thing I want you to learn from this book: *how to make the right decisions that will result in your financial freedom through operating a home-based business that's right and personally satisfying for you.* That's the perfect business.

I'm not going to teach you how to get rich as a writer, speaker, and business consultant, although you can apply the information to that end if you wish. A career that's been good for me isn't necessarily going to be good for you. I'm not going to teach you how to write a business plan or master the mechanics of running a home office, because that material is readily available. Besides, I've never had a business plan, and most of the time my office could be much more efficiently run. Nor, finally, am I going to teach you specific techniques for success in direct-mail selling, multilevel marketing, real estate, 900 numbers, or any of the myriad of "make money from home" opportunities that you see advertised in the media. But I will teach you the mind-set that can bring you enormous success in any of them.

What I know is what it takes to become financially independent by operating a one-person, home-based business in today's economy. And that's what I will share with you in the following pages. Some of that knowledge is timeless and some of it is unique to the information age. But all of it is essential.

Each of the 12 chapters covers an area of crucial importance. In brief, these are the 12 topics covered:

1. Would you like to own the greatest moneymaker in the world? Well, I have good news for you. It's free and it's yours. Read Chapter 1 to learn what it is and how to make it work for you.

2. In Chapter 2 you'll discover some interesting insights and keys to succeeding on your own that you never learned in school. Much of what we learn in school teaches us to be successful working for others but not for ourselves. I'll point out some of the major differences between what it takes to become successful as a jobholder and what it takes to become

successfully self-employed. This chapter alone will save you a lot of time and frustration.

3. If you're considering the possibilities of working from home, Chapter 3 provides guidelines for choosing a business that's right for you. You'll also find this chapter useful if you already work from home but want to make a change in what you're currently doing. I'm not going to recommend a specific business—that's your choice. But I will give you some questions and pointers to help you find a good fit for your abilities and interests. This is your most important business decision of all.

4. Want to increase your earning power? Here are two simple keys: become an avid learner and an effective communicator. This has always been true but it's truer today than ever. Chapter 4 will give you some simple but effective ways to polish both skills.

5. The survival and prosperity of any business depends on winning and keeping customers, and yours is no exception. In Chapter 5 you'll learn how to think like a marketer, spot business opportunities, and create visibility without spending a small fortune on advertising and promotion. In fact, I'll give you some ideas on how you can be paid to market yourself.

6. Thinking like a marketer, spotting opportunities, and attracting attention in the marketplace are all important, but they are meaningless unless customers buy what you're selling. In Chapter 6 you'll learn how to use personal networks and referrals to build your business, close sales, and turn those sales into repeat and lifetime customers.

7. Great ideas attract great sums of money, and that's what Chapter 7 is all about. I'll teach you where great ideas

come from and show you how to find, think up, and evaluate new, moneymaking ideas for your home-based business.

8. The most precious resources of your home-based business are your time and energy, and you have to make the best use of both. When you're running the whole show, it's easy to become exhausted, sidetracked, and frustrated and thus get little done. But it doesn't have to be that way. In Chapter 8 I'll give you some key time-management strategies that have worked very well for me and will work for you.

9. Mastering the tools of the information age is another crucial ingredient to running a successful home-based business. These tools can be a big help or an enormous drain on your time, money, and energy, depending on how you use them. In Chapter 9 I'll give you an overview of today's smart tools and some ideas for making them work for you.

10. How do millionaires get to be millionaires? What do they do? How do they live? And, most important, how do they think? That's what you'll learn in Chapter 10. Some of the information may surprise you. We will take a look at the millionaire mind-set and at some of the money strategies and tools that anyone can use to become a millionaire.

11. While you may run a one-person business, the fact is that nobody does it alone. You need customers, suppliers, mentors, professional colleagues, and advisers to make your business succeed. In Chapter 11 you'll learn how to choose the right partners and work effectively with them to help you realize your dreams.

12. Finally, you need pointers for managing yourself and staying the course when things get tough. When you run your own show, no one tells you what to do or what's an acceptable level of performance. And you need the two crucial ingredi-

ents that every major success requires—patience and persistence. Nobody said it's going to be easy. But the important thing is that if you stay the course, the success and freedom you want will be yours. In short, you have to learn how to be your own best boss, and that's what you'll learn in Chapter 12.

Correctly applied, the information in this book may well be the only 12-step program you'll ever need. To get the most from the book, read it with a highlighter or pen in hand. Make notes to yourself in the margins and write down ideas of crucial importance to you. Keep the book handy as a ready reference for your home-based business so you can use it to help you make the right decisions. For example, Chapter 10 will be useful for making financial decisions, Chapters 5 and 6 will be useful for making marketing decisions, and Chapter 11 will be useful for choosing business associates such as suppliers and advisers.

But most important, I want you to take this information and *make something happen.* To act on what you learn is all that really matters.

Is a home-based business the perfect business for everyone? Of course not. If you aren't a self-starter, it's not for you. If you need someone to tell you what to do and when to do it, it's not for you. If you abhor the thought of not getting up and going to work in a big company, it's not for you.

But if you want more time for your family, your friends, and yourself, the home-based business route is hard to beat. Although it's wonderful, the biggest payoff from running your own show isn't becoming a millionaire or even a multi-millionaire. It's the freedom, the challenge, and the enormous self-satisfaction of personal and business growth. The money is simply a means to an end and a way to keep score. By having the courage to start, you begin immediately to reap the rewards of going it on your own. When I worked for others I had hobbies. Today my work *is* my hobby. I think that says it all.

In summary, *The Perfect Business* is about getting you from where you are to personal and financial freedom earned from your own home and on your own terms. But before you begin the journey, I want to share three key values with you that I believe in very deeply. They're the foundation that my work and my business are built on. Here they are:

1. There is only one success—living your life your way.

2. There is only one negative stress—not to feel in control of your life.

3. There is only one failure—when you quit trying to realize your dreams.

If you share these values, you'll find *The Perfect Business* approach to personal and financial freedom enjoyable and profitable. And the sooner you start, the sooner you'll be free to live the life of your dreams.

1

The Greatest Moneymaker in the World

Self-conquest is the greatest of all victories.

—PLATO

Imagine that you're home alone one afternoon, fall asleep in your easy chair, and begin to dream. In your dream you meet someone who gives you the greatest moneymaking device known to man. It has the potential to create an enormous and unlimited amount of wealth for you.

The stranger gives you the moneymaker at no cost. But he hands it to you with a serious look and warns, "Read the manual first. The moneymaker is a two-edged sword. Use it correctly and you'll become wealthy beyond your wildest dreams. Misuse it and you'll encounter nothing but misfortune and poverty. It doesn't come with a warranty and you can't return it. But with proper maintenance and use, it will only get better. Good luck!"

The stranger vanishes and you wake up, disappointed to realize that it was only a dream. Damn! It seemed so real! You were given the solution to all your material problems and, in an instant, reality took it away.

No, it didn't. The truth is that you already own a moneymaker. But unlike the moneymaker in your dream, your moneymaker is capable of much more than just making you rich or poor. It can make you happy or sad, literally take you anywhere you want to go, and allow you to create the life of your choosing. In fact, that's what it has been doing for your entire life. You see, the real-life moneymaker is your mind.

Unfortunately, the real-life moneymaker doesn't come with an owner's manual. And that's one reason why it's so often unused, misused, and abused. Most of us just don't realize how much potential is lying dormant between our ears. So we take this tremendous gift for granted, use it for relatively small jobs, and consider it a cruel twist of fate that a few people have so much while many have so little. We rationalize the wealth of others with statements like:

- They're gifted.
- They're a special case.
- They have all the right connections.
- They were in the right place at the right time.
- They inherited money or can't-miss opportunity.

And let's not forget the all-time favorite, "They're just lucky." Lucky? Do you know that 80 percent of today's millionaires are self-made?

What keeps most of us from acquiring the wealth and freedom we want isn't our IQ, family history, level of education, race, sex, age, or bad luck. *It's the way we think.* Life is a game played between the ears. The way we think determines the decisions we make. The decisions we make determine what we do. And what we do determines how successful we become. Change your thinking and you change your decisions. Change your decisions and you change your behavior. Change your behavior and you change your life. Most people don't realize this. And of those who do, how many are willing to change? Very, very few. As John Kenneth Galbraith remarked, "Faced with the choice between changing one's mind and proving there's no need to do so, almost everyone gets busy on the proof."

A lot more of us would be willing to change if we only realized the freedom and riches that come with it. But that leads to a very important question: *What kind of thinking does it take to become financially independent in today's world, working in a one-person, home-based business?* That's the main question this book will answer for you. I call the answer to that question the *Perfect Business Mind-set.* With the right mind-set you'll make more right decisions, and success will follow the right decisions as surely as night follows day.

THE HEART OF THE MATTER

It's crucial that you believe and accept the following statement because it is the starting point to improving virtually everything in your life.

Your present life is the result of the choices you have made in the past. The same will be true of your future.

You are the sum of your choices. You are where you are today because you have chosen to be there. You may not like where you are. But if you think about it, the undeniable fact is that the choices you made put you there.

What's that? You say you didn't choose to be fired from your job? Who chose to take the job? You didn't decide to end your marriage? Who chose to get married? You didn't choose to be in that accident? Who chose to be in that place at that time? The answer is always the same. You did.

No, we don't choose to be born, and we have no choice about our biological characteristics. That's the hand we were dealt, and we have to play it the best we can. As Darwin said, "Biology is destiny." But with few exceptions, your biological makeup is irrelevant in determining success, happiness, or wealth. Becoming set for life begins with understanding your tremendous powers of personal choice and taking total responsibility for the thousands of choices you make every day.

You have what it takes to make a million from a home-based business. All you have to do is start making good decisions.

THE MOST IMPORTANT DECISION OF ALL

The most important decision that you'll ever make is the choice to take control of your mind. To do this you need to understand how it works and then decide what you're going to focus it on. What you choose to focus your mind on is critical because *you will become what you think about most of the time.* The late Earl Nightingale, one of the foremost success experts of the 20th century, called this discovery the "Strangest Secret." Many great philosophers and thinkers throughout history have repeatedly discovered and written about this same concept in different words. Here are just a few examples:

> "A man is what he thinks about all day long."
> —RALPH WALDO EMERSON

> "Our life is what our thoughts make it."
> —MARCUS AURELIUS

> "We become what we contemplate."
> —PLATO

> "The mind is everything; what you think, you become."
> —BUDDHA

> "As a man thinketh in his heart, so is he."
> —PROVERBS 23:7

Life as we know it is really nothing more than a series of thoughts. Everything you think you experience in the physical world is actually going on in your thoughts. According to scientists, no human being ever comes into direct contact with physical reality. Everything we experience is the product of what our brain and nervous system manufacture. We are watching the world on our own personal TV screen coupled with a terrific sound system and the added sensations of taste, feel, and smell. It's a great virtual-reality system.

Now, consider this:

- If your life is a series of thoughts (and it is), and
- If you become what you think about (and you will), and
- You have the power of choice (and you do),
- Then it logically follows that you can create the life you want by choosing what to think about.

The assumptions are true, the logic is airtight, and it works. It's the key to success, the key to failure, the key to wealth, and the key to virtually everything in life. Whether you realize it or not, you create the life you live through your choices and your thoughts.

I don't know why this isn't taught in school. I worked and studied in a university environment for 28 years and never heard mention of it. In fact I didn't learn it until 1984, when I first heard Earl Nightingale's tape, *The Strangest Secret*. Being a skeptic, I thought to myself, Okay, let's see if this really works. I'm going to think about becoming millionaire and start doing the things that will get me there. I reached my goal in 1991. You can chalk it up to coincidence or luck, but you'll never convince me it was anything other than choosing to focus my thoughts on becoming a millionaire. Once you've lived it, you believe it.

Most people aren't as successful as they would like to be because they don't understand how the mind works. They think that life is something that happens to them, and they see the world as a place where they're largely powerless. They just don't realize the tremendous power that lies within themselves.

It's much like the giant circus elephants that are kept in place by chaining one hind leg to a small stake in the ground. They have more than enough strength to uproot the stake. Why don't they exercise their power and just walk away?

Here's why. The elephants are first chained to the stakes when they are calves and don't have enough strength to break free. They try repeatedly, but they can't. Soon they learn that as long as they feel that tug when they try to move, they aren't going anywhere. So they quit trying and stay put. As they grow, their strength increases, but their belief about the chains remains unchanged. Mature elephants aren't held by chains and stakes. They're prisoners of their own minds. They believe they're eternal captives of the chains they could easily break, and for all practical purposes they are.

Now here's a very important question: What's holding you back from having the life you want? Is it circumstances? Or is it what you're choosing to believe about your circumstances and your power to change them? If you answered "circumstances," like the giant elephants, you're a prisoner of your own mind.

THE DIRECTOR AND THE SERVANT

How do we become what we think about? We are really just beginning to understand the tremendous powers of the mind and how it works. I'm personally convinced that mankind's last unexplored frontier will be inner space, not outer space. But one important key to understanding how the mind works lies in the relationship between the conscious and subconscious mind.

Here is a very simplified explanation of that relationship. Picture your mind as a giant iceberg floating in the ocean with only a small percentage of it rising above the surface. The small part above the surface is your conscious mind. The enormous part lying under the surface is your subconscious mind. The conscious mind is the decision maker. It's rational, logical, and judgmental, and it tells the subconscious mind what to do. In short, it's the boss.

On the other hand, the subconscious mind is intuitive, emotional, nonjudgmental, creative, automatic, compliant, totally gullible, and extremely powerful. It believes whatever the conscious mind tells it and will create whatever reality the conscious mind tells it to create. That is why it's extremely important to choose wisely what you think about, because if you think about it enough, your subconscious mind is going to create it. It may start as an illusion but, for better or worse, it will eventually be transformed into a reality.

When your conscious mind tells your subconscious, "I'm healthy, I'm happy, I'm prosperous, and there are tremendous opportunities out there waiting for me," your subconscious replies, "That's right, boss, and I'm going prove it to you." And the subconscious with enormous power turns the belief into a reality. Conversely, when the conscious says, "It's a hopeless, cruel, unfortunate world out there," the subconscious replies, "That's right, boss, and I'm going to prove it to you." And once again the subconscious with its enormous power turns the belief into a reality.

Your subconscious couldn't care less whether you're rich or poor, happy or sad, loved or unloved, physically fit or in poor shape. It will create the life you think about, but it doesn't care what kind of life that is. In effect, your subconscious tells your conscious mind, "Hey, boss, you want wealth? We've got wealth. You want poverty? We've got poverty. You want happiness? Coming right up. You want misery, poor health, laziness, ignorance, incompetence? You name it. It's all in stock and we deliver."

Put another way, life is a self-fulfilling prophecy. You don't always get what you want, but in the long run you'll get what you expect. My friend Jack Collis, an Australian author and speaker, put it best in his book, *Yes You Can*, when he wrote:

Life is a self-fulfilling prophecy and as you think so shall it be. You create the life you have by the power of your thinking. You will be as successful as you can imagine and believe. You will be as happy as you think you should be and you will be as rich as you are willing to settle for. This is the ultimate truth of all life.

HIGH EXPECTATIONS

Despite the finest efforts of experts to complicate matters, the master key to achieving success is simple. We become what we think about and we get what we expect. So becoming set for life begins with focusing our thinking on what we want to become and raising our expectations. In short, we need goals and faith.

Whether it's a vision, a written goal, or a formal business plan, you need some way to focus your thinking on what you want to become. You can do or become almost anything you want, but you can't become everything you want. There isn't enough time or energy for that. So you must choose very wisely and focus your thoughts and efforts.

Assuming you're well focused, how far you go depends on what you expect from yourself and from life. Centuries ago, the great artist Michelangelo warned, "The greatest danger is not that our aim is too high and we miss it but that our aim is too low and we reach it." Unfortunately, most of us are conditioned from childhood to aim low and to expect little from ourselves or the world. As children, most of us were told, "Don't get your hopes too high and you won't be disappointed." In other words, don't expect much. So you don't expect much and you aren't disappointed. But you don't get much, either.

You cannot hope to achieve exceptional wealth, health, or virtually anything else unless you aim high. The late Sam Walton, founder of Wal-Mart, became the richest man in America. His formula for success: "High expectations are the key to everything." What do you expect from yourself? It's an important question, because what you expect from yourself is the single greatest factor in determining how successful your life will be. Most of us, like the giant chained elephants, simply don't know our own strength. The fear of failure holds us back. As Mark Twain remarked, "Thousands of geniuses live and die every year undiscovered—either by themselves or others."

Whatever you expect from yourself, expect more and you will achieve more. Your self-image will improve. And an improved self-image increases your capacity to reach even greater heights of achievement and satisfaction.

When speaking about General Douglas MacArthur, Franklin Roosevelt remarked, "Never underestimate a man who overestimates himself." Although he probably meant that as a commentary on MacArthur's ego, it makes a good point. The greater our self-image, the more we expect from ourselves and the more success we enjoy.

But in addition to believing that we're capable of becoming more, we have to believe that when we become more, life will offer us more. Perception creates reality. For example, when I began my teaching career in 1969 at the University of New Orleans, I noticed a very pessimistic attitude around campus and the city that went something like this: "There's no opportunity in New Orleans if you're a woman or a member of an ethnic minority or you don't have the right connections. It's all a matter of whom you know. So if you want to be successful, move to Atlanta, Houston, Dallas, or somewhere else because you can't make it here." My colleagues and I called it the "New Orleans Syndrome," and I still hear it today.

I must admit that I was starting to believe it was true. Then something very interesting happened. In 1975 the Vietnam War ended, and a number of Vietnamese refugees settled in the New Orleans area. They were a minority. Most were broke. They weren't American citizens. They had no connections whatsoever to the business or political powers. And most of them couldn't even read, write, or speak English. If there ever was a seriously disadvantaged minority, this was it. But by the early eighties, many Vietnamese families owned nice homes and successful businesses. Their children were graduating from high school and college, many as valedictorians and honor students. And some were already financially independent. How could this happen in an area where there was no opportunity?

Again, perception created reality. The Vietnamese didn't

think, There's no opportunity here because we're a poor, dis-advantaged minority and don't know the language. Instead they thought, What a country! There's no war. We won't get shot or killed. Our homes and businesses won't get burned. We've landed in the richest nation in the history of the world! There's free enterprise and unlimited opportunity. Are we lucky or what? We can do some good here. Let's go to work and make it happen! And they did.

The major difference between the Vietnamese refugees and many native New Orleanians was simply one of percep-tion. There's never hope or opportunity if you choose not to see it. Think about opportunities and you find opportunities. Think about obstacles and you run into obstacles. As an old saying goes, "Two men looked through prison bars. One saw dirt and the other saw stars." Once again, it all goes back to choice. You will see what you choose to see.

You may be thinking, That all sounds fine. But:

IF I ALREADY OWN THE GREATEST MONEYMAKER IN THE WORLD, HOW COME I'M NOT RICH?

It's a good question with several possible answers. Perhaps you aren't using your mind correctly. Have you specifically decided what you want to become? Are you thinking about opportunities or obstacles? Do you hold high expectations for yourself and the world? Success of any kind begins with the right attitude.

What's the right attitude? I describe it as one of grateful ex-pectations. Always be thankful for the blessings you have and what you have been able to achieve. Take good care of those who help make your success possible and tell them how much you appreciate them. But at the same time, expect more and better things to come from yourself and to your-self. An attitude of appreciation and positive expectancy at-tracts success like a magnet.

But despite what all the positive thinkers and motivational

experts tell you, just having the right attitude isn't enough. It's only a starting point. It takes a lot more than that. To make a million from home requires the following:

1. The belief that you can do it. Perception creates reality.
2. The desire to do it. No one can give you that. It's totally up to you.
3. The right map to guide you and the right vehicle to get you there. The map is this book and the vehicle is the business you choose to create.
4. The self-discipline, patience, and courage to do whatever it takes until you get there.

In short, achieving financial independence takes attitude, desire, expertise, action, and persistence. With that mind-set and those attributes, you are unstoppable.

2

What No One Ever Taught You

Johnny Carson: "How did you like school?
Yogi Berra: "Closed."

The story goes that a university president told his deans, "Be nice to the student who makes straight A's because someday he may come back and teach for you. And be extremely nice to the student who drops out because someday he may come back with a million-dollar endowment." I don't know if the story is true, but it contains much more than a grain of truth.

Education is wonderful stuff. It's been my life's work in one form or another. But the fact is that just about all formal schooling prepares us to work for others. Think about it. The message we get from parents, teachers, and society in general when we are growing up goes something like this: "Go to school. Make good grades. Get all the education you can so you can get a good job." With very few exceptions, most of us haven't been taught how to be successfully self-employed.

In the school and job worlds, success depends on how well you play follow-the-leader. The leader tells you when to show up, gives you work to do, and imposes deadlines and acceptable standards of performance. If you show up and do your work well without causing any unnecessary disruption, you're rewarded in school with good grades, promotions, diplomas, and special recognition for outstanding work. Similarly, the job world rewards you with a salary, fringe benefits, promotions, interesting work, friendships, and recognition. In short, if you were successful at playing the school game, you're well prepared for the job game. You know how to be a good follower, and that's important in the job world. But the odds of making a million working out of your home by being a good follower are almost zero.

The first thing you need to realize is that success in the job and self-employment worlds involves different journeys requiring different maps. Too many start-up businesses fail simply because their owners continue to think and act like employees. You can have a great self-image, high expectations, a positive attitude, and steely determination. But you aren't going to get rich by following the wrong map. There are major differences between the job and self-employment maps, and some common misconceptions may be holding you back. One of the biggest of those misconceptions is the belief that you aren't the entrepreneurial type. So let's begin by taking a look at the new breed of today's entrepreneurs who are starting and running successful home-based businesses.

WELCOME TO THE WORLD OF THE MICROPRENEUR

It's been said that we are living in the age of the entrepreneur. And for most of us, the word *entrepreneur* brings to mind a bold risk taker who sets out on his own with the hope of striking it rich and making a dream come true. He or she takes on enormous debt, hires employees, and works endless hours. John D. Rockefeller, Thomas Edison, Henry Ford, and Sam Walton were all classic and very successful entrepreneurs. Millions of other men and women who own shops, factories, restaurants, and a myriad of other small businesses are also traditional entrepreneurs. Through the creation of jobs, goods, and services, American entrepreneurs collectively built the greatest economy in world history. I have tremendous admiration and respect for these captains of industry and shudder to think where we would be without them.

But most of today's home-based businesses, including mine, weren't started by traditional entrepreneurs. They were started by a new breed of entrepreneurs that I call micropreneurs. And micropreneurs usually have a different type of personality from traditional entrepreneurs. They come from different backgrounds, have different values, and go into business for totally different reasons.

It's important that you understand the difference between these two types of business owners. If you're thinking, I just don't have the type of personality to go into business for myself, you may believe that you have to be a traditional entrepreneur. In today's world, that's not the case. Let's look at three major characteristics that distinguish the micropreneur from the traditional entrepreneur.

Micropreneurs Are Well Educated

The English writer Somerset Maugham wrote a story about a man who worked as a janitor at St. Peter's Church in London's Neville Square until a vicar at the church learned that he was illiterate and fired him. Without a job, the man took his small savings and started a tiny tobacco shop. Over time his business grew, and he parlayed his earnings into a chain of tobacco shops worth a small fortune.

Years later his banker said to him, "You've done well for an illiterate, but where would you be if you could read and write?"

"Well," he replied, "I'd be the janitor of St. Peter's Church in Neville Square."

Like the janitor, many traditional entrepreneurs start their own businesses because they have no choice. No one will hire them, or they face a lifetime of working for others at a low wage. They start their own businesses because that's their only shot at living the good life. As a result, many amass fortunes far greater than those of well-educated employees who spend their lives working in someone else's business.

But this isn't the case for most micropreneurs. They tend to be well educated and highly employable. Many hold advanced and professional degrees. And the decision to go out on their own isn't thrust upon them. Rather, it's a choice they make.

The Primary Motive of Micropreneurs Is Freedom

Traditional entrepreneurs enjoy growing a business into a small or large empire. They want branch offices and stores. They want buildings named after them, like Trump Tower. They want a team of employees to help carry out their dreams. They want to create a going concern that they can sell for a huge profit or turn over to their children. Speaking as a micropreneur, those goals don't interest me in the least.

To be sure, I love making money and being financially independent. But the thought of having to manage a staff, meet a payroll, and struggle with the burdens of high overhead are headaches I just don't want to deal with. Furthermore, had I done all those things, I doubt that I would be financially independent today. Not only do all those things cost money, they take time away from doing the things that make money.

For most micropreneurs, the greatest incentive to go it alone is not money. It's the promise of personal freedom, a better lifestyle, and the opportunity to make a living doing the kind of work they want to do. They're tired of the rat race, the long commutes, the bureaucracy, bosses who won't listen to their ideas, and having no time for their families.

Many employees opt for the home-based business lifestyle even when it means taking a major cut in income. They find the freedom to be a worthwhile trade-off. And many a traditional entrepreneur has gotten rid of his office and his staff and moved his business home for the same reason.

Micropreneurs Aren't Big Risk Takers

Let me tell you a story. One day almost 20 years ago, I suddenly got fed up with being a college professor and thought to myself, "To hell with all this academic freedom and tenure. I'm tired of having a cushy, lifetime job. I need more challenge. I'm out of here." The following day I quit my job cold turkey and decided to write books, consult, and speak professionally, not knowing where my next paycheck was coming from.

So much for fiction. That story is almost totally false. The only true part is that I had a nice position as a tenured professor, and if there's any such thing as job security, that's it. To paraphrase the classic line from *Love Story*, Tenure means never having to say you're sorry.

The truth is that when I started my business, I didn't even realize that it would take me down a totally new and wonderful career path. I just hoped to supplement my income by writing a book, because a professor is supposed to write a book at some time in his career. I had no lifetime dream of becoming an author. It was the furthest thing from my mind. Things just started falling into place, and I decided to invest my time and energy in a new career that was more personally satisfying to me. After seeing my work published in magazines and newspapers around the world, I was no longer content to write scholarly articles for *The Journal of Unreadable Obscurity*.

Success didn't come overnight. It was six or seven years before I was making enough money from writing, consulting, and speaking to have comfortably left my university job. But I didn't resign my professorship until ten years after my first book was published. To call me a bold risk taker is, to say the least, one hell of an overstatement.

While most micropreneurs don't enjoy the job security of a tenured professor, they tend not to be big risk takers for the same reason that I had. They don't take stressful risks because they don't have to.

Why borrow huge sums of money if you don't have to? It's possible to start a home-based business with little or no capital.

Why quit your day job and live like a pauper if you don't have to? You can start building a home-based business in your spare time. If you're working 40 hours a week, what are you doing with the other 128 hours?

Why hire a staff if you don't have to? Many clerical and routine office tasks can be outsourced more cheaply or handled with today's "smart tools."

Looking back on it all, my only initial risk was investing my time and energy in the first few months on a project that might not pay off. That hardly qualifies me as a high roller.

It's common business knowledge that the greater the risks, the greater the rewards. Indeed, playing it too safe has the poorest payoff of all. But it's been my experience that success as a micropreneur comes from taking not big risks but calculated risks. This means choosing opportunities with high potential payoffs and little to lose. You can't become set for life by avoiding risk, but you can minimize your risk by choosing the right opportunities.

THE MIND-SET FOR SUCCESSFUL SELF-EMPLOYMENT

You don't have to be a bold risk taker or endure unending hardships to make a million from home. I'm living proof of that and so are countless others. To be sure, whatever business you choose to undertake will require hard work, patience, and sacrifice. There's no free lunch. Let's face it. If it were easy, almost everyone would be financially independent instead of only 1 American in 20. But you do have to adopt a mind-set that's markedly different from the one you need to be a successful employee. Let's look briefly at six main differences between the employee and entrepreneurial mind-sets.

1. Focus on Opportunity Instead of Security.

This is the toughest mind-set to adopt because we instinctively seek security. First we seek it from parents, blankets, and teddy bears. Then from teachers, role models, and peers. Then from spouses and employers and the government. And always, we want God to take care of us. From the cradle to the grave and beyond, we desperately want someone to provide for our basic needs and keep us from harm's way. But the problem with seeking security is that it doesn't exist. Security is a state of mind, not a reality. You may feel secure or insecure, but once again, perception creates reality. What you think you are is what you will become.

People who fall into the security trap pay an enormous price for their illusion. The days of giving your heart and soul to a big company in return for job security are over. If you doubt that, talk to any of the 3,000 people being let go each day in corporate America. And if you're counting on the government to take care of you in your old age, good luck. Your Social Security check will provide little more than a very, very basic subsistence.

The reality is that life is an insecure state. You can fall deathly ill at any moment. You can die at any moment. You can go broke or lose anything you've ever counted on at any moment. We all come into the world penniless and leave the same way. So if you're concerned about security, take heart. The unborn and the dead are totally 100 percent secure, and that's how we spend all but the tiniest fraction of eternity.

When you mention the possibility of going out on your own, friends, relatives, and others may advise you to forget about it and cling to the security of a paycheck, paid health care, sick leave, a pension plan, and all the rest of it. If and when that happens, ask yourself this: Are they financially independent from their work? Are they living their dreams and the kind of life you would like to lead? If your experience is anything like mine, the answers will always be no. They mean well, but like most people, they're caught in the security trap.

I'm not advocating throwing caution to the winds. Indeed, having a job can reduce the stress of making the transition from employee to micropreneur. You need to take advantage of every resource you have, and a stable job is an excellent resource. But if you hope to become set for life, your job should be thought of as a transitional resource, not as a security blanket. When you find yourself passing up or not seeking opportunities to do what you really want to do because of your job, you're most likely caught in the security trap.

You beat the security trap by having a concrete plan to leave your job by a certain date, or sooner if your business is earning enough income. Give yourself a year, two years, five years, or whatever amount of time you need to phase out of your present employment and into full-time micropreneurship.

Then start focusing on learning the skills and seeking the opportunities that will make you set for life. There are more opportunities to get rich than you could go through in a million lifetimes, and you only have one. Most people never see or capitalize on them because of the illusion of security. And that leaves even more opportunities for you.

Real economic security is generated from within. It comes from knowing that you know how to spot, create, and capitalize on opportunities. When you master that knowledge, you take a giant step toward financial freedom.

2. Focus on What Sells Instead of What You Know.

A common belief of a well-educated professional is, "I get paid for what I know." And if you're a doctor, lawyer, professor, engineer, teacher, accountant, or other professional, that may be the case—if you're employed by others. But it's an arrogant and very dangerous attitude when you're on your own.

The truth is that the success of *any* business isn't determined by what anybody knows. It's determined by what sells and how well it sells. Once you're a micropreneur, it isn't what you know but what your customers buy that counts most.

Lose sight of this one simple truth and you're courting economic disaster.

I once heard a successful business owner ask a marketing professor why no courses in sales were offered at the university where he taught. "We don't teach selling because it isn't academic," was the professor's snide reply. In 20 years of working in a university, I heard a lot of bonehead statements, but that one takes the prize. That's like a medical school professor saying, "We aren't concerned with health and healing because it isn't academic." Show me a working person unconcerned with sales, and I'll show you someone on a salary.

This isn't to say that educational credentials and knowledge aren't important. Indeed they are. Your knowledge and expertise may be key reasons why your customers buy from you. Your credentials may be a legal requirement for the work of your choosing. So be it. Just don't ever lose sight of the fact that *selling is job number one when you're a micropreneur.* Here's a little equation you may want to keep in mind: Knowledge + Credentials – Sales = Bankruptcy.

3. Focus on Getting Results Instead of Following Routines.

When Woody Allen remarked, "Showing up is eighty percent of life," he must have been thinking about life in the job world. In most jobs, particularly those in large organizations, success depends far less on the results you produce than on how well you follow the written and unwritten rules. Show up on time, put in your hours, be loyal to your boss, do the work you're assigned, and the paychecks follow on schedule. It's very predictable, but, like civilization, it's very artificial.

In contrast, consider the world of nature, where survival is 100 percent dependent on results. A hungry tiger in the wilderness doesn't get fed for pursuing his prey from nine to five. When he makes a kill, he eats. When he doesn't, he starves. If he's a good hunter, he prospers. If he's a poor hunter, he's history. There are no time clocks, no charity, no sick leave, no paid vacations, no points for trying hard, and no kissing-up. Mother Nature is an unforgiving, no-non-sense, 100 percent results-oriented bitch of a boss.

But what if that tiger is born in captivity and his owners are Siegfried and Roy? In this environment he learns, like most employees, that being well fed comes with the territory. Instead of being results oriented, he performs the show-business routines his masters teach him. Turn him loose in the jungle without teaching him to hunt, and his days are numbered.

Like the tiger in the jungle, the micropreneur has no choice but to be results oriented. Putting in long hours means nothing. Being well organized means nothing. Knowing the right people means nothing. Following a daily regimen means nothing. Being efficient means nothing. You can do all those things and still go broke.

Results are everything. You either close the sale or you don't. You make a profit or you don't. You keep your overhead low or you don't. You get paid or you don't. Your customers come back or they don't. Welcome to the jungle. But while it's sometimes cruel and unforgiving, many of us find life in the entrepreneurial jungle far better than life in the confines of employment. Like the tiger in the jungle, you know that freedom and success are yours if you do the right things. When was the last time you saw a tiger trying to get into a zoo?

Am I against following rules, routines, and regimens? Absolutely not—as long as they contribute to getting results. Just don't let them become ends in themselves. When that happens, the tail of your business ends up wagging the dog.

Efficiency is doing a job right. Effectiveness is doing the right job. Effectiveness means results, and when you're a micropreneur, results are everything.

4. Focus on Earning a Profit Instead of Earning a Paycheck.

The job world is more predictable than the self-employment world, particularly when it comes to income. If you're a salaried employee, you know with almost complete accuracy how much money you will earn in the next year. With such predictability, the typical employee mind-set becomes one of earning to spend. You work hard, get your regular paycheck, and use it to buy as many goods and services as you can afford. Thanks largely to credit cards, many of us buy a good deal more than we can afford. But if you try to run a home-based business with a paycheck mind-set, you're destined for big-time money problems. There are several potential pitfalls, and one of them is sure to do you in.

The first one is the assumption of predictability. Revenue in a home-based business is rarely predictable or smooth. It's feast or famine. One month you hit the mother lode, and the next month you come up empty. Some years will be fat and others will be lean. No matter how hard you try, there is no way you will ever have complete control over how much money your business brings in. Assuming that sales will always be there has gotten many a micropreneur in trouble.

Then there's that obscene little problem called overhead. Overhead isn't a four-letter word. It's back-to-back four-letter words. It consists of all the expenses of running your business, such as salaries, rent, utilities, supplies, advertising, equipment, and costs of the goods or service you provide. Overhead is like a dinosaur sitting on your front lawn. If you don't keep *T. rex* on a tight leash, he's going to smash your home-based business to bits. People who start a business underestimating the expenses of overhead are in for a very rude surprise.

Finally, there are all the expenses your employer automatically deducted from your paycheck that you didn't have to think about, like health insurance, Social Security, and federal and state income taxes. You have to think about them now. Ignore them and you stand to lose a whole lot more than your business. Without health insurance, a major illness strikes a double blow to your business. First, you can't work, which greatly curtails or eliminates income. And second, the cost of a major illness can put you so deeply in debt that you may never financially recover.

As for taxes, you have to think about them, too. Ignore the charlatans hyping books, tapes, and seminars on how you can legally pay no taxes. I recently heard one of them on the radio promoting his wares. During the course of the interview, he admitted to having spent the last several years in a federal prison for tax evasion. Enough said.

As a micropreneur, you need to focus on profits. It's common to hear people make statements like "We did a half-million last year." This means absolutely nothing. What was the overhead? If their overhead was a half-million, they broke even and worked for nothing. Where I come from, that's called slavery.

The profit mind-set is simple: Keep your sales high and your overhead as low as possible. Budget for taxes, health insurance, and the like. You have no control over the tax or insurance rates. And you don't have total control over your sales. However, you do have complete control over one very important item. Repeat after me:

I have total control over how much I spend.

It's crucial that you be an absolute miser when it comes to overhead, particularly in the early years of your business. Work diligently to keep your fixed expenses as low as possible. Fortunately, this isn't difficult to do in a home-based business. And it's a habit that will greatly increase your chances of becoming set for life.

5. Focus on Trying New Ideas Instead of Avoiding Mistakes.

"Don't make mistakes." That's a message we learn repeatedly from the time we're old enough to understand. In school, the person whose test has the fewest mistakes makes the best grade. In sports, the team that makes the fewest mistakes usually wins. And at work, we learn that the fastest way to do a job

is to do it right the first time. It's great advice—when the rules
and procedures are clearly defined and the right answers are
known. But that's not the environment of a home-based business. The problems you encounter cannot always be solved by
following the rules. The options are many and the answers to
important questions are unknown. The only way to truly find
out if something will work is to try it.

How do you know if your customers will buy your great new
product idea before you invest your time and money in developing it? You don't. How do you know if that marketing
campaign you're about to spend a small fortune on will pay
off? You don't. How do you know if your partner in a joint
venture will live up to his end of the bargain? You don't. Running a home-based business is an endless journey into un-
charted waters. If you wait for someone to give you the right
answers, you'll wait forever, and waiting pays very poorly.

Instead of waiting, resolve to make the best decisions you
can, try out new ideas, learn from the results, and keep trying. An anonymous philosopher described his formula for
success this way:

> *Success is the result of making good decisions.*
> *Good decisions come from good judgment.*
> *Good judgment comes from experience.*
> *Experience comes from bad judgment.*

Does this mean that you should consciously try to make
mistakes? Of course not. The best way to learn is from the
mistakes and good fortunes of others. And it's always less expensive to learn on someone else's nickel.

But don't expect to be perfect, and don't let the fear of
making mistakes keep you from experimenting with new
ideas to improve and grow your business. Every mistake and
setback carries the seeds of future successes if you are smart
enough to look for and learn from them. IBM founder Tom
Watson's formula for success was to double your number of
failures. George Bernard Shaw remarked, "When I was a

young man I found that nine out of ten things I tried didn't work. So I did ten times more work." Trial-and-error learning is a major key to home-based business success. Those who never make mistakes usually end up working for those who aren't afraid to.

6. Focus on the Vision Instead of the Short-term Payoff.

Thinking long-term is a rarity in today's world, where instant gratification is the norm. Most people in the job world get up and go to the office every day in return for a paycheck, interesting work, and the opportunity to interact with people they like. They give little thought to what their career and work life will be like in five, ten, or twenty years. They assume that whatever happens to them is something over which they have little or no control. If you start a home-based business with that attitude, proceed at your own peril.

We have an enormous amount of control over our future if we take charge of it and don't resign it to the winds of fate. Let me give you a personal example. On New Year's Day 1980 I was a fledgling writer with one book recently published and another scheduled for publication. I remember asking myself, What would you like your life to be like in 1990? I can't say that I had any specific answers, but I had a good general picture of how I wanted my life to be. By 1990 I wanted to have several more books in print. I wanted to have my own one-person operation, writing books, speaking professionally, and consulting with businesses. I wanted to be a former university professor, free from the bureaucracy and the petty politics of academia. And I wanted to have enough money put away to be financially independent. That was my vision of the good life—the freedom to do as much or as little work as I wanted, operating from the comfort of my home.

Ten years went by, and one day in 1990 I realized that all those things that I had envisioned in 1980 had come to pass. Damn! I thought to myself, It worked! I hadn't had a business plan but I had had an overall vision of where I wanted to be in 1990 and how I was going to get there.

Being able to think long-term is a strength of my friend Somers White, a Phoenix, Arizona-based financial consultant who has made millions from home. As Somers puts it:

I think successful people look a little further down the line. Unpleasant things won't destroy your productivity if you focus on your long-range goal. Success is a matter of deciding who's going to be in control. I program myself for success every day so I can make the day successful, then the week, and so on. The next thing you know, your life is a success just like you planned it to be.

What's your dream? What do you want your life to be like ten years from today? What kind of work do you want to be doing? Where do you want to be living? What kind of income do you want to be making? What do you want your net worth to be? Get a clear picture of it in your mind's eye and focus on it frequently. Then resolve to do something every day that will contribute to making that dream a reality. If your experience is anything like mine, it will pay off handsomely.

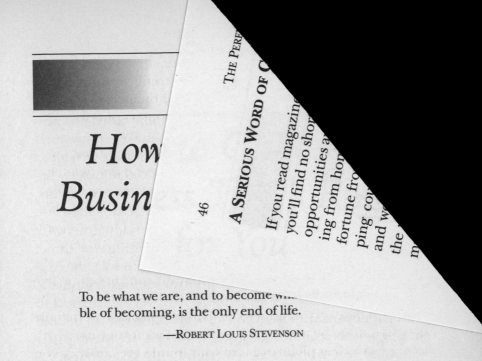

How
Busin

A SERIOUS WORD OF C

If you read magazin
you'll find no shor
opportunities a
ing from hon
fortune fro
ping co
and w
the
m

46

> To be what we are, and to become wi...
> ble of becoming, is the only end of life.
>
> —ROBERT LOUIS STEVENSON

If you're going to drive from New York to Los Angeles, you prepare in several ways. First, you have to have an accurate, up-to-date map to help guide you there efficiently. But, just as important, you want to make sure that your vehicle is capable of getting you there in good time and in an enjoyable way.

Your journey to financial freedom is very similar. You have to start off with the right map and the belief that you can get from where you are to where you want to be. But you also need a vehicle that's capable of getting you there in good time and in a way that's satisfying to you. In short, you have to choose a home-based business that's right for you. But first:

AUTION

...es, listen to the radio, or watch television,
...tage of people selling home-based-business
...d information on how to make money work-
...e. Common promises are that you can make a
...m stuffing envelopes, getting a 900 number, clip-
...pons, placing ads, reading books, making crafts,
...rking with your personal computer. Others tell you
...road to riches lies through mail-order selling, network
...arketing (also known as multilevel marketing), or direct
sale of their products. The list could go on endlessly. And
while many of these advertised opportunities are legitimate,
some, unfortunately, are little more than veiled attempts to
wrest money from those who can least afford it. As the old
cliché goes, "If it sounds too good to be true, it probably is."

How do you protect yourself from being taken? First, do
your homework. Call your local Better Business Bureau or
your state's attorney general's office and ask if any complaints
have been registered against the company in question. Call
the National Fraud Information Center Consumer Assistance
Hotline at (800) 876-7060 to report or inquire about a potential work-at-home scam. Ask to speak to several people who
have been in the business for over a year and to see concrete
evidence of how much money they are actually making.

Second, ask yourself, What do I have to lose? For example,
let's assume someone on television is offering a home-study
course on how to get rich in real estate or make money at
home with your personal computer. If the offer comes with a
no-risk, money-back guarantee, you have nothing to lose but
time and shipping costs. Similarly, if a marketing company
wants you to place a small product order to join its network,
you have little to lose. But if you have to put up several thousand dollars or purchase a large inventory of someone's products, an alarm should go off in your head.

Third, give yourself time to think things through before
committing your time and money to any venture. It's com-

mon for people who are looking for new career opportunities to go to rallies and seminars promising great business opportunities. All too often, the sponsor's true objective is to whip the audience into a mass-buying frenzy and get them to commit their money to a "one-time-only special offer." DON'T FALL FOR IT. Legitimate business people don't operate that way.

Finally, face reality. There is no easy way to financial independence. To be sure, there are many legitimate business-information sources and opportunities for sale. Some people have gotten rich buying and selling real estate. Others have become wealthy through direct selling, mail-order selling, and network marketing. And it's possible to make large sums of money working at home with your PC. While all of these businesses may be right for someone, the issue is whether or not they're right for you.

So if you're looking for someone to tell you what business to get into to make a million dollars, wake up. You're following the wrong map! You're still playing follow-the-leader. No one can tell you what business is right for you and I'm not about to try. But here's a strategy to start you thinking in the right direction:

PASSION + PROFITABILITY = WEALTH

Look for a business that allows you to do what you love, but realize that doing what you love is only half the battle. The other half is providing what customers want and are willing to pay for. In other words, becoming set for life is one part doing what you love and one part doing what's profitable.

People who achieve high levels of business success usually have several things in common. First, they have a passion for their work and a strong belief in its value. This gives them the enthusiasm to do their work every day and the zeal to persist no matter what happens. Second, they are well focused. They know where they're going and how they're going to get there.

Third, they have a natural aptitude for what they do, and they work hard to develop and polish their God-given talents. In short, they know what they're doing, enjoy what they're doing, and believe in what they're doing. Your choice of business should fit you in exactly the same manner. Doing what you love to do is very important.

But it's equally important to realize that hard work, passion, focus, and belief in your work aren't enough to make you a millionaire. You have to choose a business with the profit potential to make you a millionaire. It has to provide products and/or services that customers want to buy. It has to generate a net income over and above your living expenses that you can save and invest until you accumulate a million dollars. And you have to learn how the business works and commit yourself to continuous improvement. You have to keep learning and improving because it's a rapidly changing world, and if you don't learn and improve, you will fail. In other words, if you're going to be the owner and operator of a very successful business, that business is going to be a very large part of your life. That's doing what's profitable.

But choosing a business just for its profit potential is usually self-defeating. If you dislike the work, you won't spend the time and energy that it takes to make you set for life. And simply believing that you can become a millionaire by following your passions is naive. The world is filled with starving artists, writers, actors, and others who spend their entire lives doing what they love for a pittance. So remember the formula. Choose a business that you can feel passionate about *and* that has good potential for profitability.

If you're considering the possibility of working from home, you probably have at least a fair idea of the kind of work that you would like to do. I'm not going to give you a profile of the best 25, 50, or 100 home-based businesses. There are entire books devoted to that subject, and I recommend that you read them. Paul and Sarah Edwards have written two excellent books on the subject: *The Best Home Businesses for the 90s* and *Making Money With Your Computer at Home.* Two other excellent books that profile home-based businesses are *199 Great Home Based Businesses You Can Start (and Succeed in) for Under $1,000* by Tyler G. Hicks, and *Million Dollar Home-Based Businesses* by Sunny Baker and Kim Baker. These books may give you several home-based-business ideas that you might otherwise have overlooked.

But your best home-based-business ideas will probably come from you. And they will stem from who you are and what you have done. But keep in mind that although choosing a business that's right for you is a major and important decision, it's not cast in stone. There may be more than one business that's right for you. You can probably be successful at any number of them, and you can always pick another one if you don't like your first choice. So don't be afraid to make a decision, and get started.

Here's a five-step process to help you come up with a business that's right for you and launch it in the right direction:

1. Find Your Passions.

The author D. H. Lawrence said it best: "It is our business to go as we are impelled." While the mind is the greatest moneymaker in the world, passions are the greatest motivators. So begin by finding work that you feel is important and intrinsically interesting. And once you find it, strive every day to become excellent at it, and you're guaranteed a successful and enjoyable life. It may or may not make you wealthy, but it will make you successful.

When the great cellist Pablo Casals was 95 years old, a young reporter asked, "Mr. Casals, you're ninety-five and the greatest cellist that ever lived. Why do you still practice six hours a day?"

"Because I think I'm making progress," was Casals' reply. He was clearly a man who was following his passion. The activity of improving as a cellist was of sufficient interest and importance to him that he was willing to devote six hours a day to it.

What are you passionate about? If your reply is, "I'm passionate about getting rich working from home," that's the wrong answer. Those are *consequences*, which will probably come to pass only if you find something of sufficient interest and importance to keep you motivated for a long time. Comfort and luxury are great. But what we need most of all is something to be enthusiastic and excited about. There's a lot of truth to the old axiom that there is no labor in a labor of love.

Here's an exercise to help you discover your passions. Choose a time and a quiet place where you can think without being interrupted. Then read the following questions and write down your answers.

Imagine that you're financially independent. You have all the money you will ever need to lead a happy life.

- What would you stop doing that you are doing now?
- What would you keep doing that you're doing now?
- What would you like to learn more about or become an expert in?
- What would you do to make the world a better place?
- What would you like written about you in your obituary or said at your funeral? Keep in mind that we make a living through what we get but we make a life through what we give.
- What would you do if you knew you couldn't fail?

Consider your hobbies and interests.

- What hobbies, interests, or activities have you engaged in that made you lose complete track of time?
- What was so absorbing to you about these activities?
- What hobbies or activities were you most interested in as a teenager?
- Can any of your hobbies become home-based businesses?
- What activities can you do, talk about, or study endlessly without becoming bored?
- What's your idea of a perfect day?

What kind of work or business lifestyle would you prefer?

- Would you like to work at home, work away from home, or both?
- How much contact with people do you need? None? A little? A fair amount? A lot? Continuous?
- How much privacy do you want?
- How much do you want to work with your hands? With people? With ideas?
- Are you a goal person or a process person? Put another way, do you get your greatest satisfaction from setting goals and reaching them or from being immersed in a continuous flow of activities?

Don't censor your thoughts. Allow them to run free. There aren't any wrong answers to these questions. What you are really doing is examining your preferences, which will point the way to your most passionate interests. Whatever business you choose, it's important that you be internally motivated and are doing what you want to do.

After you have answered these questions, brainstorm as many business ideas as you can think of and write them down. This is your master list. And the only criterion at this stage is that the business be one that you feel passionate about and would have a lot of fun doing. As John F. Raynolds, chairman of Ward Howell International, Inc., put it, "The saddest people are those who say they'll work hard and enjoy themselves when they retire. Those are the guys you find facedown in the cornflakes."

2. Capitalize on Your Strengths.

I once heard the late psychologist and father of behavior modification, B. F. Skinner, define happiness as "doing what you're good at." Thanks to a combination of your natural aptitudes, your education, and your work experience, you have developed a number of unique strengths that can likely be applied to make you set for life. Your job is to discover and put them to work.

Some years ago, the Gallup Organization studied over 250,000 high achievers from all walks of life and concluded that the greatest levels of achievement occur when people are matched with work that builds on their unique strengths. Common sense? Yes. Obvious? You bet. But most of us don't build on our strengths. Instead, we spend enormous amounts of time trying to compensate for our weaknesses while our strengths go largely ignored and underdeveloped. It's probably a throwback to our school years, when we spent little time on the subjects that came most easily to us and more time trying to make a decent or passing grade in the subjects we found difficult. Later, in the job world, most performance appraisals encourage us to spend time shoring up our weaknesses.

While such a strategy may get you graduated or promoted, it won't make you financially independent. According to the Gallup study, weaknesses should only be addressed when they hinder your productivity or self-esteem. Otherwise, ignore them and spend time developing your strengths.

Successful corporations know that a major key to sustaining success is to build their businesses around one or a very few core competencies. Take a similar approach as a micropreneur. Look within yourself for something unique that you do so well that customers would be willing to pay for it. By building a business on a unique core competency, you give yourself many of the advantages of a monopoly.

Unfortunately, it's easy to overlook your strengths. They seem so natural to you that you probably take them for granted and don't think they're anything special. Have you noticed how gifted performers and athletes make their work look so easy? It's because they work very hard at developing a talent that comes as naturally to them as breathing. And that's what you need to do: *Work very hard at something that comes easily and naturally to you.*

How do you find your strengths? Begin by writing as many

answers as you can to this question: *What do I do better than most people?* Your answers will suggest a good business fit that will allow you to express your unique talents. People don't get frustrated from overwork. They get frustrated when they don't have an outlet for their natural aptitudes and abilities.

Next, look at your present job or a job you enjoyed in the past. You probably chose it because it's at least a fair match for your abilities and aptitudes. Is there a home-based business you can get into that will utilize those talents? Will your present employer allow you to work at home and hire you on a contract basis? Have you learned something or acquired a skill in the job world that could be turned into a home-based business? I know a doctor who is making a great second income teaching physicians and other professionals how to market their practices.

Finally, talk to the people who know you best. Sometimes they can spot talents that you're totally unaware of. It never occurred to me to write a book until a university colleague and friend took me to lunch one day. He told me that I had a unique writing style and should write a book on time management. No one had ever told me that, and I was 35 years old at the time. His suggestion ultimately changed my life and started me on the road to a wonderful career and financial independence.

Now go back to your master list. Have you come up with any new ideas for a business you would enjoy that had not occurred to you earlier? If so, add them to the list. And look at each business on the list in the light of your personal strengths. If you feel you don't have the skills, the aptitudes, the knowledge, or the desire to learn what it takes to be excellent in the business, scratch it off the list. Everybody can be a star at something, and you can, too.

3. Assess Marketability.

Passion and talent are great, but you'll become a millionaire only by applying them to produce something that people will pay handsomely for. That's what marketability is all about. Business success comes from providing what customers want.

Creating value is the key. What do people buy? *Benefits*. Customers exchange money for something they believe will satisfy them more than the money they have to pay for it. So whatever your choice of business, your basic job is to offer a product and/or service and convince customers that it's worth far more to them than the money it costs. That's called creating perceived value.

For example, when you go into a bookstore, why do you buy a particular book? Some possible answers might be:

- I'm interested in the subject and want to know more about it.
- A friend recommended it.
- I have read other books by the same author and liked them.
- I thought it would make a great gift.

But regardless of the reason, the bottom line is that you bought the book because you felt it was worth more to you than the money you paid for it. Otherwise, you wouldn't buy it. That's an example of perceived value.

But that leads to another question: What do customers perceive as valuable? In general, people exchange their hard-earned money for only two kinds of benefits:

- Good feelings
- Solutions to problems

Some businesses, like the one owned by oil-well firefighter Red Adair, sell solutions to problems. Other businesses, like the Walt Disney Company, Inc., sell good feelings. Most businesses sell a combination of both. Solve your customers' problems and make them feel good about the transaction, and success is sure to follow.

How *much* people are willing to pay you for what you do depends on the following three considerations:

- What you do
- How well you do it
- How difficult it would be to replace you

The more strongly people want what you offer, the more money you make. The greater the number of people who want what you offer, the more money you make. The bigger and more difficult the problems you solve, the more money you make. The higher the quality of your products or services, the more money you make. The more that people enjoy buying from you and using your products or services, the more money you make. The fewer competitors you have, the more money you make. In short, money follows demand.

From the marketing standpoint, your ideal business is one in which customers love buying from you, and/or you solve their problems. For example, Red Adair made millions of dollars putting out oil-well fires because he was one of the very few people who could solve a very big problem. To the oil companies, his services were worth far more than the fee they paid him. Disney has created one of the world's most successful entertainment empires by supplying products and services that are outstanding, unique, and bring happiness to millions every day. On the other hand, an unskilled laborer is typically paid poorly because the problems he solves are simple, and he can easily be replaced by another worker or a machine.

Where Most Home-based Fortunes Are Being Made

I cannot recommend a specific business for you because this is a choice that you and only you can make. However, I can tell you what types of home-based businesses are most likely to make you a millionaire in the shortest amount of time. Here's a very important idea to remember as you select and work in your home-based business:

There is money in information and service.

If your financial goal is to accumulate a net worth of a million dollars in a reasonable length of time, you need a business that will net you a yearly income of over $100,000. According to working-from-home experts Paul and Sarah Edwards, the following home-based businesses have a significant number of people earning six-figure incomes:

- Bill auditor
- Business broker
- Business-plan writer
- Advertising/marketing copywriter
- Desktop-video producer
- Executive searcher
- Export agent
- Home inspector
- Management consultant
- Professional practice consultant

While all those businesses are different, what they have in common speaks volumes. All are information or service businesses.

Welcome to the information age. The marriage of computer and communications technologies has created a whole new business world, where the game is played by different rules. In 1991 companies for the first time spent more on computers and communications gear than they did on industrial, mining, farm, and construction machines. In 1994 a new automobile typically contained $675 worth of steel and $782 worth of microelectronics.

What's important about the shift from an industrial to an information economy is this: Creating wealth in an industrial economy generally requires large amounts of capital and energy. I'm sure you've heard the old cliché, "It takes money to make money." That cliché is obsolete. In the information age you can create relatively large amounts of wealth with little or no capital and energy. In today's economy, providing information and delivering service are the new keys to wealth.

The ten types of six-figure businesses listed above are making money for one simple reason: *They provide their customers with information and/or services that are worth more to the customers than the fees they're charged.* That's why so many of us gladly pay for the services of a good tax accountant, financial planner, attorney, or physician. Their expertise and ability save us time and money and prevent or solve major problems. Again, their value to their clients is worth far more than the money they charge. And your choice of business should do the same for your customers. Producing and selling a product might be the right choice for you. But the benefits of selling information are hard to beat, because the profit potential is high, and the overhead is low.

Now, go back and look at the lists you made of your passions and strengths, then answer the following questions:

- What kinds of information and services would you enjoy providing that would be more valuable to your customers than the money they would pay you? Can you do or teach them something that will:
  - Make or save them money?
  - Save them time?
  - Boost their self-esteem?
  - Make their lives happier, healthier, or more successful?
- What good feelings and solutions to problems have you learned to provide in your current job or jobs you've had in the past?
- Can any of these be adapted to create a home-based business?
- What services would you like to perform that most people cannot or do not want to do?

Now, look again at your master list of potential businesses. Have you thought of any new businesses that you have the desire and aptitude to do that would be marketable? If so, add them to the list. And scratch off any businesses that you feel lack serious market potential. If you want to be successful, you've got to be valuable to your customers. Marketability is a must.

4. Do Your Homework.

The business ideas now remaining on your master list are serious potential candidates for your home-based business. The next step is to choose the one that appeals to you most and do a thorough and objective investigation into it before committing yourself.

How you pick the one that suits you best is totally up to you. For some, it may be the business with the highest profit potential. For others, it's the one they would find most fascinating. For still others, it might be the one that would consume the least amount of time. Just pick one business idea. But if you have the time and inclination to investigate two or three of them, by all means do so.

Once you identify a potential business you may want to get into, do your research. Read and learn all you can. Talk to people who are in it. What's the profit potential? How much start-up capital is required? Is the market overcrowded with businesses of this type? Is there a unique niche (an unmet need or want) in the market you can fill? How long does it take to grow the business until it is making a livable income? How will you pay your bills during that time? Can you keep your current job and start the business in your spare time? Does it have million-dollar potential? What's the long-term outlook for this kind of business? What are the downsides and unpleasant parts of the business? Every business has them. Make sure the unpleasant aspects are ones you can live with. The good times take care of themselves.

Finally, before deciding to launch your new business, check out the legal aspects of running it from home. More specifically, check the local licensing and zoning ordinances. If a business license is required, get one. As for zoning, it can be a real problem because many of our zoning laws are woefully outdated. They were written at a time when only a tiny fraction of the labor force worked from home. In 1994 more than 43 million Americans (that's over one-third of the labor force) worked at home full-time or part-time, and the number is growing by about 5 percent each year.

The acid test of whether or not you're likely to encounter zoning-ordinance problems can be found by answering the following question: *Will the business change the character of the neighborhood in any way?* More specifically:

- Will trucks be pulling up to the premises to make drop-offs or pickups?
- Will large numbers of customers create parking or other problems?
- Will the business create any kind of appearance, noise, or odors that would not normally be found in a nice residential neighborhood?

If the answer is no to all of these questions, you're not likely to have zoning-ordinance problems. From the legal standpoint, the best home-based business is totally undetectable from the street. But if your business is going to create neighborhood disruptions of any kind, check the zoning laws and make sure you're in compliance with them. Enlisting the services of a local attorney to make sure you're in compliance can prevent a lot of future headaches.

If your local zoning laws prevent you from running even an undetectable business from home, you can still circumvent the bureaucrats. Get a business address at one of your local postal and shipping services, such as Mail Boxes Etc. The cost is low, and your business address can read like this:

John Doe
XYZ Company
1234 First Street, Suite 5678
Your Town, Your State 77777-5678

The street address is that of your local postal service (not the U.S. Post Office), and the suite number is your postal box number. With so many people working from home, let's hope the laws are soon changed to conform to today's realities.

5. Focus, Focus, Focus.

Business writers and consultants are in almost total agreement about the importance of writing a formal business plan when starting a new business. While it does no harm to do so, I have never had a formal business plan. And I don't think you really need one for a solo business unless you're trying to borrow money.

But you do need to be well focused.

How do you focus on your business without a business plan? First, select only one business and concentrate your efforts on making it successful. Trying to run several types of businesses in the hope that one will pay off is likely to be an exercise in frustration. You need to focus your time and energy like a laser and concentrate on turning a single business idea into a going concern.

Second, write a mission statement for your business. A mission statement describes the purpose of a business—why it exists in the marketplace. Every business exists to serve some end user or customer in some capacity, and that's the mission of the business. Your mission statement should consist of one or a few concise sentences that answer these questions:

- What business am I in?
- Who are my customers?
- How do I create value for them?

For example, my mission is to create information that helps people work smarter. It's a broad but well-defined mission. It doesn't define me as an author, management consultant, professional speaker, or producer of audiocassette programs. Those are just vehicles that allow me to carry out the mission. It also defines my potential customer base—companies and people in the world of work. And it states that I create value for my customers by teaching people to work smarter, with the implied benefit that they will lead more productive, satisfying, and happy lives. Write a mission statement that describes the same aspects of your business.

Third, once you have a well-defined mission, create a vision statement to remind yourself of what's most important as you work in your business every day. The mission and vision of a business are not the same things. While the mission defines why your business exists in the marketplace, the vision describes an ideal picture of how you propose to carry out that mission and what you hope to achieve by it. Here's a great vision statement for a micropreneur that you may find useful:

> *My vision is to legally and honestly earn all the money I can by providing my customers with exceptional value by doing things that I can enjoy and be proud of.*

A good vision statement like that one keeps you focused on the values you should keep in mind as you work every day. The first value says it's okay to get rich as long as you do so in an ethical manner. The second value says that your job is to make sure your customers win, by giving them much more than their money's worth. And the third value says your work should be psychically enriching.

Fourth, once you have defined your mission and your values, you should have a clear, well-thought-out answer to what I call The Most Important Question:

Why did I get into this business in the first place?

What's in it for you? You need some good, selfish reasons for getting into any business, because there will be tough times. If you don't derive personal benefits from being in the business, you won't stay with it. For example, I got into the information business to have more fun and freedom and to do what I perceived as more interesting and meaningful work than I was doing as a professor. Did I do it because there was the possibility of making a lot of money? You bet I did. But even if I made the same or less money, I felt a home-based business would be more personally rewarding.

The value of being able to answer The Most Important Question is twofold. First, it will confirm that your choice of business is one that you will find personally and financially rewarding. And second, it will serve as a guidepost in the future. Once your business is a going concern, there will be turning points where you have to make major decisions. For example, you may have to decide whether to expand, enter a new market, hire someone, or take on a new line of work. Whenever you're faced with a major decision, ask yourself, Why did I get into this business in the first place? And make a decision that doesn't violate your own personal reasons for being in the business. As the popular axiom goes, "When you know what your values are, decision making is easy." Making decisions consistent with your own internal gyroscope will save you a lot of grief.

TAKE THE PLUNGE

When you know the answer to The Most Important Question, you're ready to get started. But if being in business for yourself sounds frightening and overwhelming, consider this. Most people want a job. They're afraid to go into business for themselves. Yet all of us are in business for ourselves, whether we realize it or not. Do you think a well-run business is going to pay you more than you're worth for any length of time? Chances are you will ultimately have more money and more freedom as a micropreneur.

And the odds for succeeding in your own business increase dramatically when the business is home-based. In a study of home-based business owners, Kathryn Stafford, an associate professor at Ohio State University, found that 71.2 percent of those surveyed in 1989 were in the same business three years later, and another 3.4 percent were in a different home-based business.

In another study, made from 1989 to 1992, Link Resources found that only 5 percent of home-based businesses ceased operation each year. How many people can honestly say the odds are 19 to 1 that they will be employed by their current employer a year from now? Link Resources also reported that the average household income of home-based businesses is almost twice as much as the salary of the average employee. And 20 percent of all home-business households earn over $75,000 a year.

In summary, if your home-based business idea is one that fills you with passion, allows you to use your talents, is marketable, and is well focused, don't be afraid to jump in and get started. You'll never regret it. Brian Addis, president of Wings, Inc., said it best:

Most people spend their whole lives waiting for their "ship to come in." Ships belong to those who can gather up a down payment, arrange financing for a tugboat to pull the ship into port, and hope there are only a few leaks when it gets there.

4

Two Ways to Increase Your Earning Power

If I had six hours to chop down a tree, I'd spend the
first four hours sharpening the ax.

—ABRAHAM LINCOLN

If a young person asked you, "What skills should I master to
earn more in today's business world?" what would you tell
him? I've given that question some thought and come up
with two winners. They're so simple and obvious that we tend
to take them for granted and overlook their tremendous
moneymaking potential. But I consider them my two most
valuable career skills. And the more I polish and develop
them, the more money I earn.

Regardless of who you are or what you do, these two God-
given abilities, when improved, can increase your earning
power enormously. They are:

1. The art of learning, and
2. The art of being an effective communicator.

The most successful people make the best decisions because they're the best informed. They get good information
from being avid learners. And the most successful people are

effective at influencing others to do what they want. They accomplish that by being effective communicators.

These have always been essential skills for success, but the information age makes learning and communicating more important than ever. The information age is characterized by rapid change, and in times of rapid change the learners inherit the earth. If you don't invest in learning about the latest tools, techniques, and changes in your business, the world will pass you by.

Additionally, in any information-based business, the product sold is information that can be put to a point of useful application. If it isn't communicated clearly, its value is diminished. Ever buy a piece of software with hard-to-follow instructions? Ever buy a cookbook with an ambiguous recipe for that wonderful dessert that turned out to be terrible?

Simply becoming an avid learner and a master communicator won't make you rich. Every university faculty has plenty of avid learners and excellent communicators who aren't wealthy. *The key is to focus on learning and communication skills that have a practical application. This is particularly true when you are starting your own home-based business. Choose a business and a level of wealth that will make you set for life. Then apply your reading, reflecting, listening, writing, and speaking skills toward getting the results you hope to achieve.*

Improving your ability to learn and communicate will increase your level of success and income because of a simple principle that many of us just don't seem to understand or be aware of:

You have to become more before you can earn more.

Within each of us lies the potential to become as wealthy as we want. But potential wealth isn't actual wealth any more than an acorn is a giant, spreading oak. Unfortunately, most people try to live their lives backward and wonder why they aren't successful. They want to have more so they can do more and become more. Typically, their thinking goes something like this: If I had more money, I would have more possessions, could do more things, and become more than I am. Therefore, what I need is more money. Wrong, wrong, wrong.

In reality, life works in the exact opposite way. When you become more, you can do more. And when you do more, you earn more. Becoming set for life requires investing time, energy, and money in yourself to transform your earning potential into earning power.

GET SMART OR GO BROKE

Over 200 years ago Benjamin Franklin said that an investment in knowledge pays the best interest. The difference between then and now is that it's getting increasingly difficult to make a living without continuous learning. In the old days, the world of learning and the world of work were separate entities. The schools cooked you until you were done, and then you went off to a lifetime of work. In today's world you have be continuously cooking.

You may have noticed that we are becoming a world and a nation of haves and have-nots. The middle class is shrinking while the number of millionaires and people below the poverty line is increasing. Despite what you may believe, have heard, or been told, it's not because of the Republicans, the Democrats, the government, lazy workers, greedy capitalists, unions, or competition from other nations. It's because we live and work in a global, information-based economy where knowledge is king. Those who know how to take what they learn and turn it into marketable products, services, and information grow rich. Those who don't get left in the dust. This is true for nations, companies, and individuals worldwide and it will be true for the foreseeable future. As economist Lester Thurow put it, "In a global economy you may live in a first-world country, but if you get a third-world education, then eventually you will get third-world wages."

Your chances of becoming financially independent depend heavily on your commitment to lifelong learning. You don't need advanced degrees or professional credentials unless your choice of business requires them. But you do need to master the art of applied learning and make it an integral part of your work routine.

While learning can be enjoyable and enriching, it's usually hard work, and the only reason to work hard is that you want to achieve or do something. Choosing the right sources to learn from is crucial because the ultimate aim of all this hard work and investment in learning is to make you set for life.

The good news is that there's an abundance of information about almost any business you want to learn. The bad news is that a lot of it's wrong. Here are some nuts-and-bolts ideas for finding the best information sources and sharpening your learning skills.

Ask Those Who Do It Best

This simple, commonsense idea will get you started on the right track. If you want to become one of the best in your business, talk to someone who already is. Ask him or her where the best sources of information are and what skills are most important to master. Ask questions such as:

- What are the most valuable lessons you've learned about being successful?
- What was most helpful to you when you were learning the ropes?
- What are the biggest mistakes to avoid and the greatest obstacles to overcome?
- Whom else would you recommend I talk with?
- What books and periodicals should I be reading?
- Are there any courses I should take?
- Are there any professional associations I need to join?
- What do you do to stay up to date?
- If you could give only one piece of advice to someone who wanted to do what you do, what would it be?

It's been said that a person who wants to be rich should invite a rich person to dinner and pay for the meal. Successful people in almost every walk of life are usually accessible and willing to share much of what they know. All they ask is that you have a sincere interest and that you not take too much of their time. But one word of caution: Have the common courtesy to ask questions of someone you don't plan to compete with directly.

Learning allows you to profit from other people's experiences without incurring the pain. Anytime you can learn from other people's mistakes and good fortunes, do so. Personal experience can be a great teacher but learning *only* from experience is for fools. So, when you're trying to master something new, ask those who do it best. It usually costs little or nothing. They can direct you to the right sources and spare you from the pain of mistakes you would have made, and you'll probably come away with an abundance of great new ideas.

Become a Smart Reader

Here's another simple but overlooked concept: *Your learning effectiveness is directly tied to your reading effectiveness.* According to information experts, 80 to 90 percent of the information you receive comes from reading.

There's a lot of truth to the old saying that leaders are readers. Almost without exception, the one quality that highly successful people have in common is a thirst for reading. It seems paradoxical that in the middle of the information age, so many people cannot or will not engage in the one activity that could immeasurably improve their lives—reading. As Mark Twain noted many years ago, "The man who doesn't read good books has no advantage over one who can't." Simply becoming an avid reader won't make you rich, but becoming a smart reader will equip you with a lot of the knowledge you need to become rich.

The single greatest key to smart reading is selectivity.

Knowing what to read and what to ignore is far more important than how fast or how frequently you read. For example, if you read at the average rate of 250 words per minute, knowing not to read a 100,000-word book will save you almost seven hours of reading time. By applying selective reading techniques, you can quickly get a good overview of a book or article and decide if reading it in detail is worthwhile. Here are some strategies for smart reading:

1. Make smart reading a regular part of your work routine. Set aside a specific amount of time each day, week, or month for professional reading and applied learning. Large, successful companies like Corning and Motorola are requiring that all employees spend a minimum of 5 percent of their time on the job in training and learning new skills. This mandate is imposed simply because the investment in time and money is enormously profitable. Motorola estimates that every dollar it spends on training generates $30 in productivity gains within three years. There is no reason why your learning efforts can't have just as healthy a payoff.

2. Always evaluate your reading in light of your goals. Before deciding to invest your time in reading a book or article, ask yourself, What do I hope to learn from this that will help me become set for life? If you don't have a good answer, move on to something else.

3. Preview books and articles before deciding to read them in detail. Before buying or reading a book, look at the subtitle and read the information on the jacket. This will give you a good overall feel for the book and the author's credentials. Check the publication date. Is this recent information? Read the table of contents and scan the preface. Pick out a page at random and read it. Would this information be beneficial to you? Look through the book and read the subheadings in the chapters. Is the book organized and written in a clear, easy-to-comprehend fashion? If so, it's probably a book worth

investing your time and money in. If you see only a chapter or two that will be useful to you, resolve to read only those chapters and put the book aside.

Similarly, you can preview articles of interest before reading them in detail. Look at the title and the topic first. If it looks useful, scan the article, reading the first sentence of each paragraph. Anything of help here? If so, read it. If not, send it to the round file. Once again, selectivity is the key.

4. Highlight reading material that you will refer to again. This will drastically cut your rereading time. Get in the habit of reading reference or how-to materials that you will read again with a pen and/or yellow highlighter in your hand. Make notes in the margins. In addition to cutting your rereading time, looking for the most important points to highlight will improve your comprehension.

One very successful business owner I know has come up with a great system for getting the most from the books he reads. He highlights the most important points and gives the book to his secretary. She types the highlighted sentences, producing a summary of the key points of the book for quick reference. He also gives the summaries to his employees, saving them reading time while giving them useful information.

5. Resolve to read a book, magazine, or article by a certain date or get rid of it. Don't allow your reading material to pile up. If you do, the odds are you'll never catch up, and you aren't going to get ahead by reading yesterday's information tomorrow. Treat your reading material as if it were a movie playing at a local theater. If you don't see it by a certain date, it's gone, and if it's something special, it will be back.

6. Once you master the previous strategies, you can improve your reading effectiveness by increasing your reading speed. Rapid-reading courses claim their students read at thousands of words per minute. In fact, they're skimming the material for overview rather than reading for detailed com-

prehension. Simply because so many of us have poor reading habits, however, a good rapid-reading course can double or triple our reading speed and increase our comprehension.

If you move your lips while reading silently, have to hear each individual word in your head as you read, or backtrack and reread certain sentences, you have faulty reading habits that can be corrected with practice and guidance.

You can improve your reading speed on your own by practicing some of the techniques taught in rapid-reading courses. Practice reading a phrase at a time rather than reading word for word. Take in larger eyefuls and force yourself to scan more rapidly over the material. Don't reread; just keep pressing ahead. It may seem uncomfortable at first, but with practice, your speed will improve.

Finally, if you find your reading time is severely limited, other options are available to help you. First, there are services that publish short summaries of the best business books. For the modest price of a subscription, you receive several book summaries each month. Some services provide written summaries. Others provide summaries in both written and audiocassette form.

And speaking of cassette programs, they're another excellent learning vehicle. The beauty of cassette learning is that you can learn from some of the finest minds in the world while dressing, driving, shopping, cooking, or exercising. But don't make the mistake of thinking that you can learn all you need to know from cassette programs. Use them as a supplement and not as a substitute for reading.

Overcome Learning Obstacles

It's been said that the mind is like the stomach. What counts isn't how much you put in but how much it digests. Locating the right sources and improving your reading effectiveness will put more and better information into your mind. But unless you can fully grasp the material and put it to work, you're wasting your time.

Whenever you have trouble understanding what you're trying to learn, it's probably due to one of three common learning obstacles. Here is a description of each and some ideas for removing them:

1. *Unfamiliar words and terms.* This first obstacle will drive you up the wall unless you recognize it and take steps to manage it. For example, let's assume you're trying to become computer literate. The first thing you encounter is a huge number of unfamiliar terms—RAM, ROM, hard disc, floppy disc, megabytes, DOS, Windows, hardware, and software, for example—that leave you feeling totally confused, frustrated, and tempted to throw up your hands and walk away. Don't do it. Knowing how to use a personal computer is an essential home-based business skill, and the buzzwords aren't that hard to learn. It just takes a little time, patience, and persistence.

The solution to overcoming unfamiliar words is simple. Whenever you are learning a new field of knowledge or a new technical skill, make it your business to learn all the technical terms, jargon, and unfamiliar words first. If you do that, the rest of the learning will go faster and much more smoothly. If you hear or read a new word or term you don't understand, find out what it means. Get a precise definition. Write it down or look for a written definition. Find out if there's a glossary of words and expressions you need to know and make it your job to learn them first. It will save you a lot of time, energy, and frustration.

2. *Skipping steps to learning.* You had to learn to crawl before you could walk and walk before you could run. Your mental processes work much the same way. For example, you can't learn algebra without a basic understanding of arithmetic, or learn calculus without knowing algebra. Similarly, you have to know how to write a sentence and structure a paragraph before you're ready to learn how to write a report. So whenever you're trying to learn new material and you get con-

fused, go back to what you understand and move slowly forward from there. New learning is only possible if you begin with what you already know and understand.

3. *Too much abstraction.* Let's say someone recommends that you read a particular book. You begin reading it and learn a lot of terms, definitions, and concepts but fail to see how the information can be applied to help you become set for life. If that happens, call the person who recommended the book and ask, "Can you give me some specific examples of ways I can put this information to work?" If he can't give you a satisfactory answer, quit wasting your time and get back to work or find something else to read.

In summary, getting advice from those who do it best, becoming a smart reader, and overcoming learning obstacles are three key learning skills for acquiring the knowledge that will make you set for life. But most important, remember that simply learning what to do is meaningless until you put it to work. One of my all-time favorite thoughts comes from an anonymous executive who wrote:

> *To look is one thing. To see what you look at is another. To understand what you see is a third. To learn from what you understand is still something else. But to act on what you learn is all that really matters.*

THE COMMUNICATORS OWN THE WORLD

Here's another obvious but overlooked business truth. *Regardless of who you are, every penny you earn comes as a result of the cooperation of other people.* Customers are people. Employees are people. Suppliers are people. Partners are people. And people will make or break you, depending on your ability to get them to do what you want. While technical and financial skills are important, people skills are paramount.

While you can't succeed without a certain level of business knowledge, the greatest rewards go to those who combine knowledge with the ability to express their ideas clearly. But in addition to being clear, effective communicators are master persuaders. They know how to get people to do what they want.

We all know effective communicators. They're the ones customers eagerly buy from and recommend to their friends. They're the ones others bend over backward to help because they like and respect them so much. So if becoming set for life is your goal, effective communication is a skill you need to master.

Empathy and Conviction Are Essential

Learning to be an effective communicator isn't difficult. The techniques are simple. But in addition to good technique, the best communicators have two other things going for them: *empathy* and *conviction*. They know how to put themselves in other people's shoes and see the world through their eyes. They feel the joys, problems, and wants of those they communicate with. All effective communication begins with focusing on the other person and what you want him to do as a result of your message. Once you understand the other person's needs and wants, your job is to show him how he can get what he wants by doing what you want.

Just as important as empathy is conviction. The most persuasive communicators are those who feel strongly about their message and the need to share it. To quote a popular sales axiom, "People don't care how much you know until they know how much you care." The best salesperson is the one who believes deeply in what he sells and is eager to help as many people as possible by sharing the benefits with them.

Conviction is important because of two key principles you need to keep in mind. First, *people are ruled by their emotions.* Practically all decisions we make are dictated by our emotions and feelings. Look at the food you eat, the person you married, the clothes you wear, the work you do, and where you choose to live. If you think those are logical choices, think again.

Second, *emotions are highly contagious.* Listen to a group of people laughing and you want to laugh. When someone we're with yawns, we want to yawn. We watch a sad movie, and tears come to our eyes. Stories with happy endings make us feel happy. Positive people energize us. Negative people drain us.

Consequently, persuasion isn't converting people to your way of thinking. It's converting them to your way of *feeling and believing.* That's another reason why it's important to choose a business that you believe in and have a passion for. When you're sold on the value of what you do, people get much more than just the words of your message. Your beliefs and feelings come through, and that's when effective communication occurs.

How to Communicate with Impact

Communicating with empathy and conviction will make you highly persuasive. But you also need clarity to ensure that people understand your message and that you understand them. That's where good technique comes in. Here are some general communication techniques to ensure that your message is welcomed, listened to (or read), and understood:

1. Begin with the end in mind. Whether it's a telephone call, a sales call, a letter, a report, an advertisement, a media interview, or a luncheon speech, start by focusing on the results you hope to achieve by communicating. Remember, we are talking about applied business communication. If you only want to establish rapport, that's fine. Just recognize what your intended results are before you begin. Then organize your message around the points you want to make to get the

results you want to achieve. Communication is like everything else in life. The rewards go to those who know what they want and focus on achieving it.

2. Tailor your message to your audience. The more you understand the other party, the greater the odds of achieving the results you want. Who are these people? What do they want and how can you help them get it? Speak to them in their language.

3. Communicate positively. Before preparing your message, tell yourself, I'll make them glad they heard from me. Then tailor your remarks to conform to that statement. People are starving for good news. They can't pick up a newspaper or magazine or turn on the radio or TV without getting the other kind. Make your message positive, and others will pay attention.

4. Get and hold their attention. My friend Morris Massey knows the value of this. When he taught a college course in advertising, he walked into class the first day, took out a blank pistol, and shot it in the air. After the students got over the initial shock, he stated the point he was illustrating. If you want to communicate with people, you have to get their attention. If you bore them, you lose them. Practicing what he preaches, Morris has since gone on to an exceptionally lucrative second career as a platform speaker. His appearances and video tapes have made him set for life because he knows how to get and hold an audience's attention.

5. Establish trust and rapport. Give people a reason to open up, listen to, and communicate with you. What's in it for them? Are you entertaining? Can you help them or solve a problem? Why should they believe you?

In face-to-face situations, a number of nonverbal communication techniques will help create rapport. Establish good eye contact with people. Don't stare hypnotically into their eyes, or they'll think you're a nut. But make regular eye contact, especially when you're making an important point. Lean slightly forward when they speak and nod your head in agreement, indicating that you understand. Subtly mirror their rate of breathing, speaking, and gesturing. And whatever you do, don't say or do anything that might be perceived as insulting or offensive. When people are put on the defensive, communication shuts down.

Humor is an excellent way to establish rapport if it's done in a non-offensive way. For example, when I'm being introduced as a speaker, I imagine some in the audience are thinking, Oh, great, an author with a Ph.D. Sounds like a cure for insomnia. So when I get to the platform, I often begin by saying, "I'm wearing a wireless mike today. If you ever wear one, I want to give you the best piece of advice you'll ever learn about wearing a wireless microphone. Someone passed it on to me the first day that I wore one. He told me, 'Michael, turn it off if you go to the rest room.'" This usually gets a big laugh. The audiences relax, I relax, and I'm on my way to establishing rapport.

6. Use the KISS principle: Keep It Short and Simple. The shorter and simpler your message, the greater its impact. Conversely, the longer the message, the greater the odds of losing your audience. People today are very busy and have grown up with television. The result is that most people have very short attention spans. So get to the point and stay on the point. Don't use big words when small ones will do. Keep your sentences and paragraphs short. After you write a sentence or paragraph, go back and eliminate every unnecessary word. Make sure that every word tells. Verbose is morose.

Here's another tip to improve your writing. When you finish writing something, read it out loud to yourself or someone else. If it sounds good, it will read well. Strange as it may seem, the key to good writing is not the eye. It's the ear.

7. Give specific examples to illustrate your points. The best communicators are storytellers. They don't just state an abstract point. They illustrate it by giving specific examples or telling a story about how something is done or why it's important. Through examples and stories, good communicators help others to visualize, understand, feel, and believe their message.

8. Anything that conveys communication *is* communication. Your tone of voice communicates. Your choice of words communicates. The way you dress communicates. Body language communicates. Your business cards, stationery, and mailings communicate. The way your telephone is answered communicates. Look at your business through your customers' eyes and make sure you're sending out the intended message. The image you should project is of someone your customers would want to come to for advice and to help solve their problems.

9. Listen, watch, and ask for feedback. The best communicators realize that communication is a two-way process that involves sending and receiving. The worst communicators are like alligators—all mouth and no ears. When you're receiving, you're learning.

For example, did you know that a prospect is more likely to buy from a salesperson when the prospect does 80 percent of the talking? The smart salesperson doesn't just jump in and start telling the prospect how great his products and services are. He asks questions to establish rapport and listens for answers to determine if the prospect can benefit from what he's selling. If so, they discuss ways of working together. If not, he thanks the prospect for his time, asks if he knows someone who might be interested in buying, and moves on.

Anytime you can get feedback, do so. Ask your customers how they like what you're doing and how you can better serve them. Ask your suppliers, partners, and associates for ideas about ways you can work together for mutual gain.

When you're having a face-to-face or telephone conversation, give the other person your undivided attention. When someone says something important, and you want to make sure you understand, tell him, "Let's make sure I understand this." Then paraphrase what he told you and ask if it's correct. Similarly, if you want to make sure you're understood, rephrase your message and ask, "Does this make sense to you, or do I need to make myself clearer?" It's a way to find out if your message is getting through without putting the other party on the defensive.

10. Practice, practice, practice. Once you know the basics, you have the key to improving any skill. You get better by learning some very elementary principles and consciously practicing and polishing them. If you want to be a better public speaker, speak a lot. If you want to improve as a writer, write a lot. And the same holds true for improving your reading and applied-learning skills. First, learn the basics. Then practice putting them to work and strive to get better every day.

5

Magnetic Marketing: How to Attract All the Business You Need

Wealth is always attracted, never pursued.

—ANONYMOUS

Customers. They're the lifeblood of every business because without customers, you have no business. As the old axiom goes, "Nothing happens until somebody buys something." The most important function of every business is to create and keep customers. It's that simple and that difficult.

It's a common belief that most business failures are caused by a lack of capital. It's also false. Practically all business failures are caused by a lack of customers. If you have enough customers, you can do almost everything else wrong and still make a profit. But if you don't have enough customers, you can do everything else right and go broke. As humor writer Linda Perret remarked, "The customer isn't always right, but he's always the one with the money."

In a solo business, it's easy for us to think of ourselves as the business. Don't believe it for a minute. The customers are the business. We are the service providers. But if you're like I was when I started out, you probably think *sell* is a four-letter word, and you don't want to do it. Additionally, you don't have a small fortune to spend on advertising and marketing to get others to beat a path to your door. Therein lies the biggest initial and ongoing problem for a micropreneur: How do I win and keep enough customers to make a healthy profit without knocking on doors and spending a fortune on marketing? It can be done, and I know it can be done because I do it. I call the process magnetic marketing. Like a magnet, you set forces in motion that attract customers to you.

I have never knocked on doors, sent out direct-mail pieces, or called up people looking for business. I don't advertise and spend little or nothing on promotion. And all the money I don't spend on marketing stays in my pocket and directly contributes to making me set for life. It's called profit. But here's the best part: Believe it or not, I literally get paid to market myself. And that money, too, goes toward making me set for life.

Magnetic marketing isn't smoke and mirrors, creative financing, or some funny-money pyramid scheme. It's totally legal, honest, and ethical. To be a magnetic marketer all you need is the right mind-set, a little common sense, an understanding of why people buy, and the knowledge of a few simple techniques that anyone can apply to grow their business. For purposes of explanation, I've divided the process into six basic parts:

1. Get the magnetic marketing mind-set.
2. Scan your market for opportunities.
3. Create visibility.
4. Use networks and referrals to build your business.
5. Close the sale when customers come to you.
6. Service, service, service.

GET THE MAGNETIC MARKETING MIND-SET

Because most of us have been educated and trained to view work with a job mind-set rather than a self-employment mind-set, there are two widely held marketing myths that get novice business owners in trouble. Recognizing and correcting them at the outset will save you a lot of time, money, and frustration.

Myth #1: Because I Love It, It Will Sell

Let's assume you're starting a new business or have a great idea for a new product or service. It's terrific. It's creative. It's wonderful. It's unique. It's the greatest idea you've ever had! Therefore, it will sell. Right? Guess again. The problem with this kind of thinking is that you're assuming your customers have the same wants, needs, tastes, and view of the world as you do. And while that may or may not be true, to assume it's true is taking a blind and dangerous risk. You don't get rich selling what you love. You get rich selling customers what they want.

Between my junior and senior years in college, I worked at a small-town radio station in rural Mississippi. The owner spent a fortune on the station but could never make a profit. Why? He insisted on playing only the music he loved—Lawrence Welk, Guy Lombardo, and soft instrumentals. The playing of rock, country, and gospel music was forbidden because he didn't like it. Well, you can just imagine what size audience that drew in a small Mississippi town in the mid-sixties. Few people tuned in, and because the audience was small, few businesses paid to advertise on the station.

On the other hand, a nearby competing station owned the market because the owner had a totally different mind-set. He once told me, "I hate listening to my station because I can't stand the music. I just tell the manager to play what the people want, and we keep making money."

Myth #2: If I Do the Best Job, the Customers Will Come

How I wish that were true. Just do the best work and you'll get the gold star. It works in school. It works in sports. It sometimes works on the job. But in the marketplace, it rarely works. "If you build it, they will come" is from the movie *Field of Dreams*. It's not from the marketplace.

Here's the problem. In the marketplace there is no best work. There is only the perception of what is the best. What you perceive as the best work, someone else may perceive as average, mediocre, or poor work. What one customer thinks is a great value is a waste of money to another. In the real world, there's no such thing as:

- a good value or a poor value;
- a good product or a poor product;
- high quality or low quality;
- great service or poor service;
- a good deal or a bad deal.

Only the customer's *perception* makes it so.

Your success as a micropreneur won't be determined by the products or services you offer. It won't be determined by how hard you work or how many hours you put in. Nor will it be determined by your IQ, the number of degrees you have, or whom you know. You can do a great job, work hard, be brilliant, have great contacts, and still go broke. It happens every day because these factors don't determine success in business. They may contribute to success but they don't determine it. *The success of a business is determined by the number of its customers and how much they spend. And that's determined by what they think, feel, and believe about the business. Period.*

Successful marketing is a game played between your customers' and potential customers' ears. It's not what you know but what they perceive that counts. When it comes to marketing, how you perceive your business is irrelevant. How customers perceive your business is everything.

To adopt the magnetic marketing mind-set, forget about your own view of the world. Put aside your ego, your prejudices, and your opinions and look at the world through your customers' eyes. Who are your customers? What do they want? What is value to them, and how can you provide it? Answering those questions correctly is the master key to success in any business. If you have a mission statement for your business, you already have the answers.

SCAN YOUR MARKET FOR OPPORTUNITIES

Making money becomes very easy when you have the answer to this question: *What do my customers want most and how can I provide it?*

Find a need and fill it. Find a hurt and heal it. Find a problem and solve it. Find an itch and scratch it. Find a want and satisfy it. Any successful entrepreneur will tell you that the key to making money is to satisfy unmet wants in the marketplace. But as simple and obvious as that is, most new micropreneurs don't think that way. Instead of thinking, Let's find a need and fill it, they think, I'll do what I do best and get someone to buy it. But again, because value is determined by the customer's perception and not by what the micropreneurs do well, the result is a lot of hard work for very little money.

Your first priority is to find out what your customers want most. Then focus on using your passions and strengths to satisfy those wants. When customers want what you're selling, earning money becomes incredibly easy. You don't have to spend a lot of time, money, and effort hyping what you sell. You just have to position yourself in the market so customers know who you are, what you offer, and how to reach you. The result is they come to you.

Where the Big Money Is

The biggest payoffs come when you're the first business to spot an unmet want and fill it. This is true for two reasons. First, you have a monopoly until competitors discover it and enter the market. In the land of the blind, the one-eyed man is king. Second, being the first business to offer a new product or service positions you as the preeminent market leader. For example, who was the first photocopy company? Xerox, of course. Who was the second? Who cares? When requesting a photocopy, people often ask, "Will you make me a Xerox?" Have you ever heard anyone ask, "Will you make me a Sharp, Panasonic, Canon, Brother, Ricoh, Kodak, or IBM?"

How do you spot opportunities before they become obvious? Here are two questions that, when correctly answered, will keep you one step ahead of the crowd. They have served me well. The first one is:

Where's the Pain?

Find out what's bugging your customers and potential customers. Where there is perceived pain, there is a sense of urgency about solving the problem. And people pay handsomely for solutions to urgent problems. A person having a coronary doesn't negotiate the price of medical care or say, "I want to think it over." He wants the problem solved *now* and worries about the details later. That's an extreme example, but it illustrates the point.

How do you find the pain? It's simple. Ask customers, and they will tell you. A problem is the difference between what the customer has and what he wants. So ask the customer, "What do you have?" and "What do you want?" Or, to put it another way, "What is the situation now?" and "What would you like it to be?" That's how you find the pain.

Once you know where the pain is, your job is to come up with a product or service that solves the problem for a price that enough customers will happily pay to keep you in business. Having achieved that, you're on your way. Your customers' unsolved problems are your moneymaking opportunities.

The second opportunity-spotting question is:

What's the Trend?

Wayne Gretzky, professional hockey's all-time leading scorer, was asked why he was so successful. He gave it some thought and replied, "Most hockey players skate to where the puck is. I try to skate to where the puck is going." Similarly, most businesses go where customers are. But the most successful ones anticipate what customer wants are going to be and are the first to satisfy them. One way they do that is by studying trends.

Trends and fads are not the same thing. Trends are long-term patterns of change that have a major impact on our lives. Fads are short-term phenomena surrounded by great hype but that have little or no lasting impact. Pet Rocks, Pac Man, Nehru jackets, and Rubik's Cube were fads. They came and went. The growth of the information economy, the aging of the population, globalization of markets, and working from home are trends. They have been evolving for years and are making profound changes in our lives.

To be sure, no one knows what the future is going to bring. As movie mogul Samuel Goldwyn quipped, "Forecasts are dangerous, particularly those about the future." Indeed, forecasters can be incredibly accurate and hilariously wrong. For example, in the 1890s a news agency asked 74 prominent Americans to predict what the future would be like in the 1990s. Mind you, the participants were not self-appointed psychics or crackpots. They were people in positions of high authority, such as presidents of major corporations, U.S. senators, and presidential cabinet members. They got a few things right. They accurately predicted that the telephone would supplant the telegraph, be placed in every household and business, and make worldwide communication possible. They also accurately predicted:

- a forthcoming income tax;
- air-conditioned buildings and homes;
- women getting the right to vote;
- Florida becoming a tourist and retirement state;
- the growth of the suburbs.

Not bad, but here's what they also predicted for the 1990s:

- Air travel will be in balloons. (No one foresaw the impact of the automobile or the invention of the airplane.)
- The railroad will still be the fastest means of travel.
- The mail will still travel by stagecoach or in pneumatic tubes.
- The largest U.S. city will be Chicago or Denver.
- Laws will be simplified, leaving no work for lawyers. (How's that for optimism?)
- Religion will have solved the alcoholism problem.
- Crime will be minimal because criminals won't be allowed to breed.
- Unemployment will disappear.
- Marriages will be happy because incompatible couples will be executed.

Can anyone today do a better job of accurately predicting what life will be like a hundred years from now? Probably not. But you don't need to know how things will be different in a century. All you need to know is what changes are likely to occur in the next several years and how you can capitalize on them. Here are six major trends that are changing and will continue to change the way we work and live. When looking for opportunities, consider these:

1. *Think globally.* Technology is shrinking time and space. Depending on your business, your customers can be any-

where in the world. Thanks to the fax machine, some lawyers in London use typists in Taiwan because the price is lower.

2. *Think safety and home.* Thanks to crime, drugs, nuclear power, a polluted environment, terrorists, AIDS, health-care costs, distrust of our leaders, and the end of job security, people today perceive the world as a very dangerous place. As a result, many are centering their lives around the home, where they feel secure. Sales of home-security systems, handguns, water and air filters, expensive kitchens, lavish baths and bedrooms, luxury entertainment centers, and home-office equipment are all rising.

3. *Think customer convenience.* With two-career couples and people working longer hours, time is *the* scarce resource. Businesses and people are time-poor. Any product or service that saves them time and energy has great moneymaking potential.

4. *Think aging baby boomers.* Those born between 1946 and 1964 constitute the largest age group and are the trendsetters of the population. As they age, the boomers' discretionary incomes will rise, giving them even more clout in the marketplace. The health-care, wellness, recreational, entertainment, retirement, and financial-services industries will all have new opportunities, fueled by this enormous population. If you want to know where the money is, follow the boomers.

5. *Think information and service.* Because we live in an economy dominated by the need for information and services, that's where the opportunity is, particularly for those with home-based business aspirations.

6. *Think customization.* Today's customers have more knowledge and more choices than ever. If you don't give them what they want, the way they want it, when they want it, they're more than happy to spend their money somewhere else. Cus-

tomization brings customers back and virtually eliminates the competition. Find out what each customer's special wants and needs are and tailor your products and services to their liking. The extra investment in time and effort will repay you many times over.

CREATE VISIBILITY

In addition to selling what customers want, you need to get their attention and convince them that you have what they want and that you're the best person to buy it from. To do that, you have to become visible. People can't buy from you until they know you exist. But what do you want to be known *for*? Every business lives and dies by its reputation, and a good reputation doesn't happen by accident. It starts with deciding how you want others to perceive your business and working hard to communicate that perception.

Begin, as always, by looking at your business through your customers' eyes. What motives are their buying decisions based on? What do they value most when they buy from a business like yours? What can you do for them better than anyone else can? What benefits are they really buying when they buy from you? Are they buying hope? Peace of mind? Self-esteem? The lowest price? A wonderful experience? A great future? Customized service?

Then decide how you want to be perceived by answering this question: *What's the single most important feature of my business I want my customers to know about?* For example, do you want to be known for:

- Reliability?
- High-quality products?
- The finest service?
- Fast service?
- The lowest prices?
- Unparalleled expertise in your field?

- Customized solutions to customers' problems?
- Your money-back guarantee?

While you may offer all these benefits and many more, pick only one. Then write a short, original statement, phrase, or word that tells the customer why he should buy from you—the shorter the better. This is your Unique Sales Proposition, or USP. And once again, if you have written a good mission statement, you may already have your USP.

You need a USP for one simple reason. No matter what you sell, the odds are overwhelming that a lot of other people are selling it, or something very similar, too. If your business is perceived as just one of many, the odds of getting inside the customer's mind are small. Remember, there are countless other businesses competing for the customers' attention every day. Your job is to come up with a strategy to convince them that you're unique, memorable, and a better value than the rest. Marketing experts call this *positioning* your business.

Here are some well-known USPs that you may be familiar with:

- Federal Express, when it absolutely positively has to be there overnight.
- Hallmark, when you care enough to send the very best.
- Like a good neighbor, State Farm is there.
- At Ford, quality is Job One.
- Wal-Mart, always the low price, always.

If you're naming a new product or looking for a name for your business, find one that promises the benefits. For example, Carnation captured the liquid-diet-preparation market with a product named Slender. Two other excellent product names are Lean Cuisine and Dustbuster. All create a memorable image in the customer's mind, one that promises the benefits of buying the product. Whatever your USP, it should persuade customers to buy from you because you're offering them the benefits they want. Once again, this means looking at the business through the customers' eyes and knowing what's most important to them.

Once you have created your USP, every communication coming out of your business should reflect the image you want to project. Your stationery, business cards, printed materials, the answer on your voice mail, and the way you look, dress, and act should all be in sync with your USP. *You* are your business's most important advertisement. Decide how you want to be perceived and send that message.

Whom Do You Want to Receive Your Message?

To answer that important question, you should ask yourself, Who are my customers? What group of people has the money, the greatest need, and the inclination to buy what I'm selling? Do they live in a specific geographic area? Are men or women the most likely buyers? Will I be selling to specific income, educational, or occupational levels? Am I selling to consumers or other businesses? In short, you need to target your message to a specific market and create visibility in that market. Remember, visibility is only a means to an end and not the ultimate goal. The goal is to create and keep customers.

Promote Thyself

Some people go broke trying to create visibility. They spend a fortune on expensive advertising, lavish brochures, mass mailings, hiring a publicist, and telemarketing. While doing all those things may feed your ego, they aren't necessarily going to feed your bank account. Unless you're skilled in these areas, the odds are the money you spend on promotion will help someone else become set for life.

There are inexpensive ways to create visibility. There are free ways to create visibility. And you can literally be paid to increase your visibility. Here are five specific strategies:

1. Write an article and get it published where your potential customers will read it. The article should be related to what you do and give readers some information that will help them solve a problem. Finally, be sure to let them know how they can contact you. Many years ago, I promoted a time-management seminar I planned to teach by writing an article for a local publication on how to manage time effectively. The publication was mailed free of charge to the local business community. It created visibility, and the result was that my first time-management seminar sold out. My cost? Zero.

2. Volunteer to speak at luncheons and meetings that potential customers are likely to attend. Professional associations, service organizations (such as Rotary, Lions, Optimists or Kiwanis clubs), or business-networking functions are always looking for people willing to speak on topics of interest to their members. Tell your audiences how you can solve their problems. It's another way to create visibility at no cost.

One additional low-cost tip: When you speak, leave a trail of tangibles. Pass out at least one piece of printed information that the members of the audience can take with them and that includes the name of your business and how to contact you. It could be a wallet-sized card, a pamphlet, a reprint of an article you have written, or an order form. Whatever you leave, make it something that will be valuable enough to potential customers that they will take it with them and keep it handy for future use.

3. Volunteer to present a free seminar for a school or organization that stands to benefit from your offering it to their students or members. If participants include potential future customers, it's another way to create visibility at no cost. As with the speech, it's a good idea to give the audience tangibles to take with them. A psychologist who specializes in child discipline launched his practice by volunteering to speak at local PTA meetings. He gave his audiences some excellent parenting techniques, and his practice grew quickly.

4. Get interviewed on radio and TV. It's not as difficult as you might think. Talk shows are proliferating and always looking for new guests who have something to say that will attract and hold an audience. The key to making it effective is to target the shows whose listeners and watchers are potential customers.

You don't have to hire a publicist to book you on radio and TV shows. You can do it yourself, and a number of people have done it with great success. As you can imagine, getting booked on shows and being an effective guest are subjects and arts all to themselves, but if you're interested in giving it a try, read a good book on the topic first. My personal favorite is *On the Air*, by Al Paranello. The book is no longer available in stores but can be ordered for $12.95 postpaid from PO Box 279, Norwood, NJ 06478. I have personally done hundreds of radio and TV interviews and find Paranello's advice excellent.

5. Write a book to demonstrate your expertise. If it addresses a problem or subject that interests a large number of people and is well written, a publisher will buy it, publish it, promote it, and distribute it for you. Your visibility and credibility as an expert in your business will skyrocket. You'll be interviewed on radio and television shows. And instead of volunteering to speak, you'll be paid handsomely, which increases your visibility and sells more books. If you're an effective speaker, giving a good speech usually results in additional paid speeches. In short, you'll find yourself being paid to market yourself.

Writing a book is no small undertaking in terms of time and effort, but if you're serious about it, you need to know how to write a book proposal and how to approach publishers. *Write the Perfect Book Proposal*, by Jeff Herman and Deborah Adams, is an excellent book on the subject.

Those are five ways you can create visibility and promote your business with little or no out-of-pocket cost to you. Of course, they really aren't free. You're paying for the exposure with your time and with the hope that the visibility will translate into sales. In the early stages of a home-based business, most of us have a lot more time than money to invest in promotion. My experience is that it's a worthwhile investment.

6

More Magnetic Marketing: How to Network, Close Sales, and Keep Customers for Life

If you want to be found, stand where the seeker seeks.

—SIDNEY LANIER

Okay, you've grasped the magnetic marketing mind-set, spotted some great opportunities, and you're finding ways to create attention in the marketplace. Great, but it's only half the battle. The other half of magnetic marketing is creating contacts, turning contacts into customers, and turning customers into repeat customers. Let's look at three strategies for doing just that.

USE NETWORKS AND REFERRALS TO BUILD YOUR BUSINESS

Imagine the following: You've just moved to a new city that you are totally unfamiliar with. You need the services of a good family doctor, tax accountant, clothier, grocer, pharmacist, and numerous other professionals and organizations. Would you prefer to choose them on the basis of their advertising or by getting recommendations from people you trust? The answer is obvious.

When it comes to winning and keeping customers, the magic word is "trust." Basically, everybody is afraid of getting burned when they make a buying decision. Let's face it. Every industry has a few con artists and shoddy producers who are more interested in making a fast buck than building a solid business. But once people know you, like your work, and trust you, they readily come back and will gladly recommend you to others. Business is and always will be people and relationships.

Your most powerful sales force is an army of satisfied customers. Absolutely nothing sells you better than a customer telling others how wonderful your products, services, and you are. And they pay you! When satisfied customers recommend you, you're literally being paid by those who are doing your best marketing.

You may be thinking, That's a great philosophy when you have customers. But I'm just starting out. I don't have any customers, much less anyone who will say nice things about me. What do I do?

Make Them an Offer They Can't Refuse

Find people who can benefit from what you sell and who have influence among your potential customers. Every market has gatekeepers—people of influence whose recommendations carry clout. If you know them, contact them directly. If you don't, go through someone who knows both you and them and ask to be introduced.

Once you've been introduced, offer the gatekeepers a free sample of your work or a healthy discount in return for writing a testimonial letter or statement for you. You may also ask them to tell at least three good prospects about your work and what it did for them. Assure them that they are under no obligation to do anything unless they are completely satisfied with your work.

A number of them will accept your offer. And when they do, dazzle them with your best work. Keep in mind that the best work is what *they* want. Leave no stone unturned. Do everything possible to make them say Wow! Don't worry about no pay or poor pay for these early jobs. If you're selling what people are willing to pay for and doing a spectacular job, you're sowing seeds whose harvest will repay you many times over. Business isn't hunting. It's gardening. You're cultivating the relationships and forming the type of work habits that lead to long-term success.

Some of your clients may have trouble writing a good testimonial or not know where to begin. If that's the case, write up a few good working models for them to adapt as they write their own. Show them letters that others have written. Or you may volunteer to write a letter or statement for them, with the understanding that they can modify it as much as they want. This will save them time and increase the odds of getting the kind of testimonial you want.

A good testimonial letter or statement is brief and specific. It doesn't just state that you did a good job. It tells prospects how good the work was, what it did for them, and, most important, how they feel about it. For example, here are some excerpts from testimonial letters that were written to me and that I send out when a prospect contacts me about the possibility of a speaking engagement:

As a result of your seminar we will save about $1,000,000 and share a portion of that with our team members. Thanks to Dr. LeBoeuf and the Greatest Management

Principle in the World, everyone at Stew Leonard's is a winner. We love Dr. LeBoeuf!

—STEW LEONARD, JR.
Stew Leonard's
World's Largest Dairy Store

I have planned and hired the speakers for all our food and beverage seminars since 1981. During that time we have had some exceptional presentations with messages. However, none of them was delivered more convincingly or with greater sincerity. Mixing humor with a topic, delivering the message, and getting the audience to believe it is an art. The responses and discussion I have heard from the attendees clearly indicate that you succeeded one hundred percent.

—EDDIE ANDREWS, VICE PRESIDENT
MHM, Inc.—America's Largest Independent
Hotel Management Company

Absolute *rave* reviews from all of our people. You set the tone that was carried throughout all our sessions. . . . I look forward to working with you in the future.

—GORDON H. HASTINGS, PRESIDENT
Katz Radio Group

Michael, you were absolutely the best speaker we have ever had. Period! All the reps told me personally how much they enjoyed listening to you.

—DONNA GOULD, PUBLICITY DIRECTOR
The Berkley Publishing Group

Thank you so very much for the sincere and professional way you delivered your presentation at Action's annual meeting. The feedback I have received has been universally positive. One of my greatest satisfactions in business comes from contracting for goods and services—and getting what I bargained for. Never has that result been so completely achieved than in obtaining your services.

If I can ever relate our positive experience to anyone else
on your behalf, please don't hesitate to ask.

—THOMAS F. SACKMANN, PRESIDENT
Action Mortgage Company

Testimonials should be written on your customers' stationery. As you collect testimonials, store them in a binder
with plastic covers where you can easily get your hands on
them as needed. Some find it worthwhile to reprint the letters in full color to mail or give to prospective customers. And
once your business is established, keep asking for testimonials and referrals. You can never have too many people writing
and saying nice things about your business.

Reward Those Who Send Business Your Way

While satisfied customers may be your best sales force, that
doesn't mean they're the only sales force. There are lots of
other people out there who can send business your way if you
make the effort to network with them and make it worth their
while.

The concept of networking and word-of-mouth marketing
is a very hot topic in business today for one simple reason: So
many people are starting small businesses that need to find
other businesses they can work with for mutual benefit.
That's why you'll find no shortage of business, professional,
or service organizations through which you can meet other
people. The key is to pick them wisely. Choose only one or a
very few organizations that will be good for business networking and ignore the rest. Otherwise you'll spend all your time
meeting and socializing and not working. Marketing without
producing is another surefire formula for bankruptcy.

How do you decide whether or not to join an organization
or go to its social functions? Answer this question: *Am I likely
to meet people there who will buy from me or refer customers to me?* If
the answer is no, don't go unless you have some other reason
for going.

The world is full of professional joiners who never met an organization they didn't like. They go to all the meetings. They hold offices and serve on committees and boards. And since they do all that free work, the organizations love them. Nothing wrong with that. It's just that when you run a solo business, you can't delegate your work to others while you go out and play social butterfly. Your networking time needs to be marketing time. And that means putting yourself in front of customers or people who will send customers your way. With that thought in mind, here are some guidelines for networking with others for mutual gain:

1. Look for businesses that complement yours to network with. For example, put a tax accountant, financial planner, estate-planning attorney, stockbroker, and insurance agent together, and you have five people who can refer customers to each other endlessly. Similarly, a wedding photographer would find it profitable to network with caterers, jewelers, bridal consultants, florists, churches, synagogues, and reception halls. When a customer buys from you, what other products and services is he likely to want or need? Those are the types of businesses that would be excellent ones for you to network with.

2. Competitors can also be an excellent networking opportunity. Just because you go head-to-head with other businesses doesn't mean that you can't work together sometimes for mutual gain. Have you ever noticed how one airline will book you on another carrier if it doesn't have a flight to the destination or at the time you want? Airlines have an agreement whereby they book business for each other in return for compensation. You may find it useful to work out such an agreement with some of your competitors. Or you may have an informal agreement whereby you refer your competitors to customers for no pay. I frequently refer other speakers to potential clients if I can't do a date or provide the kind of ser-

vice at the price the client wants. Other speakers do the same for me as well.

3. Before going to a networking function, prepare in advance. Bring plenty of business cards. If you want to be remembered, have your picture printed on your business card and do something with your name tag that will attract attention. My friend Susan RoAne, author of *How to Work a Room*, tells of one man who drew a huge crowd by writing "Money" on his name tag. Another guy wrote "on your name tag" on his name tag because the hostess told him to "write on your name tag." It got plenty of attention.

Also before going, compose and memorize a brief, memorable statement that describes in 30 seconds or less just what you do. Refer to your mission statement and Unique Sales Proposition when writing the description. For example, if I were going to a networking function, my description would be, "I help people work smarter through my books, tapes, and seminars. My latest work is focused on teaching people how to become financially independent working in a one-person, home-based business. I know firsthand that it can be done and I want others to profit from what I have learned."

4. Once you get to the meeting, make good use of your time. Arrive early and leave late. That way you'll meet more people. Don't stand around and wait for others to come to you. Act like a gracious host. Go up and introduce yourself to others. Find out what they sell and what type of people they want to connect with. If that's not you, do you know others who might be of help to them? If so, pass their names along. Encourage others to tell you about their businesses, and you'll be remembered as a brilliant conversationalist. If you know someone who might be a potential customer for them, pass the information along. After you learn about their work, be sure to deliver the short message about your business to everyone you meet. Exchange business cards and write any-

thing you need to remember about them on the back of their card. Don't be abrupt, but try not to spend more than ten minutes with any one person. Remember, you're there to market yourself and help others. The more people you meet, the greater your chances of forming a few good, profitable relationships.

5. Be sure to ask for leads and referrals. That's why you're there. After describing your business to someone, ask, "Who do you know who . . . ?" and describe your typical customer. It may be that person, or you may remind him of someone who could be your next big customer. As you get leads, write them down and follow up as fast as possible.

6. Always remember the Great Law of Life: What goes around comes around. If you want to get referrals, you need to give referrals. Reciprocity is the basis for all good relationships, and it's especially true in business. When someone sends a customer to you, acknowledge it with at least a thank-you note. A small gift is even better. And sending him a customer is better yet. Keep in touch with those you network with. If you see an article or item of interest to them, clip it out and mail or fax it to them.

Finally, when you refer a customer to a business, make sure it's a quality business. If the customer gets poor treatment, it's going to reflect poorly on you.

Multiply Your Marketing Effort by Outsourcing It

While no business can exist without marketing, it doesn't necessarily follow that you have to do the bulk of it yourself in order to be successful. Marketing can be outsourced to others who will advertise, sell, and distribute your products or services in exchange for a piece of the action. The key is to find a company with the marketing muscle and expertise to sell what you produce and then convince that company that partnering with you is a win/win for both of your businesses.

Let's use the sale of this book as an example. I had the option of putting up the capital to publish, distribute, advertise, publicize, and sell the book myself. Instead, I took it to my literary agents, who sold the book to the publisher. For selling my book to the publisher, the agents get a percentage of all moneys the book earns. In effect, I outsourced the selling of the book rights to my agents in exchange for a piece of the action.

The publisher, in turn, produces, distributes, advertises, publicizes (with my help), and sells the book to the public and pays me a royalty for each copy sold. The odds are overwhelming that the publisher will sell far more copies than I would if I tried to do it all myself. The trade-off is that I make far less money per copy. Once again, I have outsourced much of the marketing of the book to a partner in exchange for a piece of the action. I also produce audio-cassette programs and sell them wholesale to other businesses. They, in turn, advertise them in their catalogs, send out mailings, take orders, and distribute them to the general public. Again, I'm partnering with a business that agrees to do a lot of the marketing for a piece of the profits. You can outsource the marketing of services, too. Many of the speaking engagements I receive are booked through speakers' bureaus that market me in return for a percentage of my fee.

Whether you produce a product, a service, or both, there are sure to be other people around able to market it and make it far more profitable than if you try to go it alone. Seeking them out and selling them on marketing what you produce might be your biggest and best sale of all.

CLOSE THE SALE WHEN THEY COME TO YOU

If you're selling what people want, and they know about it, they're going to contact you to find out more. When that happens, your first order of business is to determine if they are legitimate prospects. Put another way, you need to find the answer to three questions in a relatively short period of time:

1. Are you selling what they want to buy?
2. Can they afford it?
3. Are you speaking to the decision maker?

When people go to the trouble of contacting you, the overwhelming odds are that the answer to the first question is yes. But don't just assume that's the case and launch into an eager sales pitch. Instead, take a few minutes to find out more about them. If they ask you to describe your products or services, give them a brief description, much like your networking message, that will summarize the benefits.

Then ask them some questions. How did they find out about you? What's their situation now? What would they like it to be? Where's the pain? Ask questions that begin with who, what, when, where, and why to determine if what you're selling is a good fit for what they want. And find out if your price is compatible with their budget. Selling is like medical care. Prescription without diagnosis is malpractice. By taking the time to ask, listen, and learn, you're developing rapport, building a bond of trust, and finding out what prospective customers want. All of this is essential for effective selling.

If you don't feel what you sell is right for them, be honest and tell them so. If you know a business that sells what they're looking for, recommend it, thank them for thinking of you, and tell them, "I hope I can be of help to you in the future." It can be very hard to turn down money, especially when your business is new. But selling people what they don't need or can't afford is a blueprint for disaster. Happy customers tell 3 or 4 people. Dissatisfied ones typically tell 8 to 12 people, and they tell even more. Nothing will make or break you faster than word of mouth.

Finally, before you spend too much time with people who contact you, find out if they're the ones who will make the buying decision. Otherwise, you risk wasting a lot of time and energy. Many a salesperson has spent hours trying to persuade someone to buy, only to be told, "You'll have to talk to my boss. He makes the final decision." Nip that in the bud. Ask at the outset, "Are you the buyer, or will others be involved in making the final buying decision?" If someone else makes the decision, explain the basic benefits of what you offer and tactfully ask to speak with the decision maker. While you don't want to seem brusque, your time will be better spent with someone who can buy.

Find the Hot Button

Here's another key to successful selling: *People buy with their emotions and justify with logic.* We like to think that our buying choices are logical, rational, and well thought out. But, as with practically all our other choices in life, we don't choose what we need. We choose what we want and then use logic to justify our choices.

For example, people spend billions every year on diet books, exercise videos, fitness machines, health club memberships, weight-loss programs, and the like. There's a very logical reason for buying these products and services. People in good shape lead more productive, healthier lives. But there's also an emotional reason for buying. People with fit, trim bodies look much sexier. The ads for these products and services are the giveaway. Are they selling health or sex appeal? They may tell you about the logical benefits for buying. But what do the models and persons selling the products look like? Everyone in the health, weight-loss, and fitness business knows that the promise of good health isn't the hot button that causes most customers to buy. The hot button is the hope of becoming more attractive. We buy the promise of sex appeal and justify the purchase by telling ourselves that we are really buying good health.

Similarly, no matter what you sell, there will probably be an emotional benefit that motivates a given customer to buy from you. It might be your personality, your low price, your convenient location, your reputation for personal service, the recommendation of satisfied customers, or any one of a number of other things. As you ask questions and present the benefits of buying what you sell, watch very carefully for any emotional responses. Once you find the hot button, concentrate on stressing that particular benefit.

Overcome Objections

Most people who are interested in buying aren't going to buy right away. They will probably raise objections with the hope that you'll ease their concerns and persuade them to buy. It costs too much, they might say. They can get a better price elsewhere. What you offer isn't exactly what they had in mind. Why should they buy it when what they are using now is satisfactory?

Don't let objections throw you. They're a statement of interest. If you're going to make sales, you have to handle objections. Here are some strategies for doing just that:

1. The best time to handle an objection is before the customer raises it. As you sell your products or service, you will hear the same objections being raised by many different customers. Those are the objections you want to head off at the pass. For example, if you're a tax accountant, a common objection from potential clients might be, "I can do my own return and save the tax preparation fee." Show them at the outset how your knowledge of the tax laws will save them far more in time, money, and frustration than the fees you charge. If they understand the value, they can never raise the price objection.

But you won't be able to predict or handle all objections up front. So here are two other tactics for overcoming them:

2. Listen, agree, and empathize with customers' objections. If you argue with them, you'll just lose them and the

sale. Nod your head in agreement and tell them you understand how they feel. Your goal is to achieve a oneness with the
customer that lets him know that you're on his side and want
to do what's right for him. If he believes that, you'll make the
sale.

3. Eliminate the objection. If a customer says, "I can't afford it," you counter with, "If we come up with a payment
schedule to fit your budget, would you be willing to buy?" If
he says, "Your price is too high," you counter with, "If I show
you how it's worth far more to you than the price you'll pay,
would you be willing to buy?" If the answer is yes, build value
by telling him about all the benefits of the product or service
and what it will do for him. The bottom line to all objections
is this: *Customers want to be convinced that what they're buying is*
worth more to them than the money it costs. Your job is to show
them that it is. Each objection you eliminate brings you one
step closer to closing the sale.

Make It Easy to Buy and Ask for the Order

If what you sell is right for the customer, and he wants it,
you're very close to closing the sale. But you're going to lose a
lot of sales if you don't understand and take charge of the
end of the sales process.

Once the customers want to buy, a whole new set of problems and fears starts to bother them. What if your product
doesn't do what you said it will do? What if they aren't happy
with it? What if their spouse, business partner, or boss doesn't
like it? How will they pay for it? They need time to think it
over. Your job now is to reassure them and take the fear out
of the buying decision. Always offer a money-back guarantee
and you'll close more sales. Sooner or later, every business
must guarantee its work. The smart ones do it up front.

If customers are worried about affording what you have to
sell, tell them you'll work out a payment schedule or help
arrange financing that they can afford. If they're afraid it

might not work for them, tell them you have numerous satisfied customers who had the same initial concerns and are glad they went ahead. If they want to think it over, remind them of your money-back guarantee and give them an incentive for buying today. Throw in something extra or give them a discount for acting now. In short, make it easy to buy by offering a risk-free deal and a reward for acting now.

Finally, *you must ask for the business.* You don't need 101 clever lines to manipulate customers or trick them into buying, but you do need to ask politely for the order. Summarize the key benefits of what your product or service will do for them. And while they're thinking about those benefits, ask for the order. "Would you like to try it?" "When can we get started?" "I know you're going to like it. Can we ship you one today?" "Try it. You have everything to gain and nothing to lose." If you don't ask for the order, you're going to lose a lot of business. If you ask for the order, you're going to get a lot of business. It's that simple and that important.

You're going to get some refusals, of course. Don't take them personally or let them immobilize you from asking others for their business. If your business and the potential customer just weren't right for each other as the customer perceived it, be polite, thank him for his time, and tell him, "I hope I can be of help to you in the future." Ask customers who don't buy if you can check with them at a later date to see if they might be interested in buying then. A lot of today's no's can become tomorrow's yeses with tactful persistence. Ask customers if they know anyone who might be interested in what you sell and would refer you to them. With magnetic marketing, you aren't going to get nearly as many refusals as you would by cold-calling. But you're still going to get your share. It's just a part of doing business. When you get a refusal, accept it, try to learn from it, and move on.

And when you get a yes, here are the three most important words to remember:

SERVICE, SERVICE, SERVICE

When you close a sale with a new customer, it's tempting to pat yourself on the back and celebrate your achievement. That's fine, as long as you keep this thought in mind: *The closing of the sale is the opening of a relationship.* Your new job is to make that relationship so valuable to your customers that they will return time and again to buy from you and tell others about the great work you do.

The surest, fastest, and least expensive way to build your business is to take very special care of your customers. It costs approximately one-fifth as much to keep a customer as it does to get a new one. Customers tend to buy more from you for each year they stay with you. The cost of servicing them decreases for every year they stay with you. And they're your absolutely best source of advertising and marketing. The small dollars are in closing sales. The big dollars are in keeping customers. And the way you keep customers gets back to those three magic words: service, service, service.

Nothing will kill a new business faster than a reputation for poor service. Once people form an impression about your business, it tends to stick. And it's extremely tough to change a negative image in the customer's mind. That's why it's crucial that you overwhelm your early customers with outstanding quality, value, and service. If early impressions of your business are negative, it's almost doomed from the start. With that thought in mind, here are some pointers for building a reputation for outstanding service:

Reliability Is Paramount

As comedian Flip Wilson used to say, "Don't write a check with your mouth that your body can't cash." Do what you say you're going to do. Do it when you say you're going to do it. Do it right the first time and get it done on time. That's reliability, and it's the most important ingredient to building a solid reputation for outstanding service.

Responsiveness Is Crucial

If you want to lose customers, ignore them. Sixty-eight percent of customers who stop buying from a business do so because of an attitude of indifference toward them. When customers have a request, a problem, or a need for special attention, they want it dealt with *now*.

Fortunately, technology makes it possible for a solo business owner to keep on top of things very inexpensively. My 10-year-old telephone answering machine cost less than a hundred dollars and keeps me in touch with customer inquiries from anywhere in the world. I just call the machine when I'm on the road, get my messages, and return calls promptly. I once called someone when I was in Hawaii to tell him that I wouldn't be able to speak on the date he was inquiring about. As it turned out, he was so impressed that I returned his call in less than an hour from so far away that he hired me for a later date. Since that time, I've done four additional speaking engagements for that man's company.

It's also very important to respond quickly to customer complaints. Seventy percent of customers who complain will do business with you again if you resolve the problem to their satisfaction. But if you resolve the problem on the spot, 95 percent will do business with you again. Responsiveness pays.

Make Them Glad to Hear from You

Here's another simple but often overlooked truth: People like to buy from people they like. Make no mistake about it; you have to deliver the goods, too. People aren't going to continue to buy from you just because they like you. But you can be sure that they will buy elsewhere if they *don't* like you. While I don't recall the exact wording, an old Chinese proverb states that a man without a smiling face shouldn't open a store.

Every time you have any kind of contact with customers, try to make them glad they heard from you. Do they like to be entertained with jokes or amusing stories? Do it. Can you empathize and listen to them? Do it. Can you solve a problem for them? Do it. Can you pay them a sincere compliment? Do it. Can you tell them you appreciate their business and be the type of person they want to do business with? Do it. Part of good service is giving a good performance. After an encounter with an obnoxious waitress, Susan RoAne said it best: "If I want to be annoyed, I'll call my mother."

Look, Listen, and Ask for Feedback

As a popular saying goes, "A customer who complains is my best friend." Don't just assume your customers are ecstatically happy about the job you're doing for them. Find out by getting candid feedback. While you may think you're doing a superb job, it's what the customer thinks that will make or break your business. A lot of business is lost because people just assume they're pleasing the customer—as the customer quietly takes his business elsewhere. According to an old retailing axiom, "Customers don't bitch, they switch."

Basically, you need feedback to find the answers to two questions: How am I doing? and How can I get better? Try to find out as specifically as possible what customers like most about your work and where you need most to improve. Ask them one-on-one. If you aren't comfortable with that, give them a short questionnaire to fill out. Ask them to rate you from 1 to 10 in several aspects of your work, and have some open-ended questions through which they can express themselves in their own words. As you get feedback from several customers, you will see certain strengths and weaknesses mentioned time and again. Your job is to build on your strengths. If the weaknesses can be readily fixed, do it. If they can't, don't do work in those areas. Recommend someone else and do work that capitalizes on your strengths.

You also want to get feedback from customers who have gone elsewhere. Painful as it may be, it's a chance to find out why they left. The result is that you'll likely learn something valuable that will keep you from losing other customers. And by demonstrating your concern, you'll get a number of them back.

Underpromise and Overdeliver

When customers buy from you, they have an expectation about what they're going to get for their money. The key to a great service reputation is to exceed their expectations. Pleasantly surprise them. Throw in something extra that they weren't expecting at no charge. Charge them less than the initial price you quoted. If they ask you for a special favor, do it and another one they didn't ask for. You always want to leave the customer with the impression that he's getting his money's worth and then some. Make the customer say Wow! and you'll never want for business. Money flows in where great service flows out.

7

Don't Compete; Create

The factory of the information age is the human mind.

—DONNA PARTOW

Processionary caterpillars travel closely behind each other in long, continuous lines. Years ago Jean Henri Fabre, a French entomologist, led a line of them onto the rim of a large flowerpot where they formed a circle in which the leader of the procession was following the tail of the last in line. Nearby and in the creatures' full view, Fabre placed an abundant supply of nourishment for them to feed on. To discover the food, all they had to do was look around. But for seven days and nights, the caterpillars followed each other in an unending circle until they died of exhaustion and starvation.

There's a valuable lesson in that experiment for all of us in a home-based business. Instead of blindly following the crowd, step out of line, look around, and you're likely to find a lot of prosperity within your reach. Blind conformity isn't where the money is.

A popular business axiom states that you should know your competition almost as well as you know your customers. Although that may be sound advice, I've discovered a better road to success in business: *Don't compete; create.* Use your creative abilities to keep you one step ahead of the crowd. Use your imagination to think up new products and services that make your and your competitors' existing ones obsolete. Find faster, cheaper, and better ways to get things done.

In a rapidly changing business world, innovation is king. Being the first to offer the latest products and services enables you to charge premium prices, win new customers, and keep the ones you have. And finding better, faster ways to get things done improves your profits through lowering your costs. If you're doing anything the exact same way you did it last year, the odds are you're doing it wrong.

Innovation and creativity are related but different. Creativity in business means thinking up or discovering new ideas for making or saving money. Innovation is the process of turning those ideas into profitable realities. In business, creativity without innovation is a waste of time. But you can't have innovation without creativity.

Many people feel that creativity has no place in the practical, bottom-line-oriented world of business. We tend to think of it as the province of the flaky artist, the mad scientist, or the nutty professor. But great businesses are built on great ideas. *Everything* begins with an idea, and great ideas attract great sums of money. Show me a wealthy, self-made man or woman, and I'll show you someone who believes in the power of ideas.

One reason most of us don't get as rich as we could is that we use our minds for small jobs. We use them to memorize and recall facts and figures. We use them to observe, pay attention, and follow directions. We use them to make judgments, analyze, and reason. But we rarely use their most powerful capability—to imagine new ways to make us happier, healthier, richer, and more valuable to ourselves and others. Why? Because we weren't taught how. Remember follow-the-leader? Practically all schooling teaches us what to think and how to think but not how to think up.

There is no question in my mind that wealth is created by the way we think. And if you're in business, it is imperative to harness, utilize, and put to work in your business your most valuable mental ability—your ability to think imaginatively and creatively. I would remind you of the words of Albert Einstein: "Imagination is more important than knowledge."

EVERYONE CAN BE CREATIVE

Most people don't think of themselves as creative because they don't spend their days writing, painting, performing, or working on scientific breakthroughs in a laboratory. But those are just narrow applications of a universally distributed human talent. Anyone who can think can be creative. It's a God-given human ability. Some people have more creative ability than others, but everyone has some.

Studies of highly creative people reveal that they share one important common trait: *they see themselves as creative.* Consequently, they work at using and developing this part of their thought process. And because they use it, it gets better and stronger. Just as you can improve your memory or your powers of observation, judgment, and reasoning, you can improve your ability to think creatively.

If you doubt that we are born creative, spend some time with small children before they go off to school. Notice the incredible imaginations they have. If they don't have a playmate, they create an imaginary one. A stick becomes a gun, and a dollhouse becomes a palace. Notice the unending number of questions they ask. Unbridled imagination and curiosity are two important creative abilities all of us are born with.

But then the children go off to school where they learn what and how to think. Memorize that poem for a test next week. Learn that formula for getting the one right answer to the problem. We spend years developing our powers of memory, recall, observation, judgment, and reasoning, while our ability to think imaginatively and intuitively goes largely ignored. Is it any wonder that most of us don't think of ourselves as creative? To be sure, the other mental powers are important, and we need to develop and use them. But it's also important to realize that they're no substitute for creativity.

Another reason many of us don't use our creative capabilities is that we think being creative means coming up with an idea that's totally or completely new. *Nothing* is totally new. New ideas are no more than new combinations of old ones. New melodies are new combinations of existing chords and notes. New books are new combinations of existing ideas and words. New paintings are new arrangements of color. New products and services are new combinations of existing ones. Put Oreo cookies and granola bars together and you get Oreo-flavored granola bars. Add home-delivery service to pizza and you have a simple idea that founded an entire industry. Combining old ideas to create new ones is the essence of creativity. And it only takes one good idea to make you rich.

Creative thinking isn't magical, mystical, or complicated. It doesn't take advanced degrees or a high IQ. It's really very simple, and anyone can do it. What it takes is awareness and the application of some simple strategies and techniques for thinking up and discovering new ideas.

STRATEGIES OF SUCCESSFULLY CREATIVE BUSINESSES

Businesses known for creativity and innovation practice a number of simple strategies that you as a micropreneur can adapt to your own business. Here are the ones that have worked well for me:

Make a Commitment to Creativity and Innovation

When you're in business for yourself, you need to understand that your future success depends on your ability to come up with new products, new services, and new ways to get things done. Unless you do this, the world will pass you by. As a micropreneur, your research-and-development department is your ability to think creatively about your business.

One way that large, innovative companies commit themselves to innovation is by requiring that a minimum percentage of sales comes from relatively new products and services. For example, the 3M Corporation and Johnson and Johnson require that at least 25 percent of all revenues come from products less than five years old. Rubbermaid requires that 30 percent of revenues come from products less than five years old. And over half of Hewlett-Packard's sales come from products less than three years old.

This is a simple concept that you as a micropreneur can adopt to keep your business committed to staying on the edge. Set a goal to derive a minimum percentage of your yearly sales from new products and services, and work toward achieving that goal every year. While it will be automatically attained in the early years, striving to meet an innovative goal will keep your business from getting stale as years go by.

Create and Innovate from Your Core Competencies

As a micropreneur, you have to choose a business that builds on your strengths. These are your core competencies. Here's another strategy from the big companies that you can apply: Find your core competencies and use them to create something unique.

For example, 3M's core competency is applying a layer of a closely controlled material to a flexible base. As a result, some of their creative innovations have been masking tape, magnetic tape, cellophane tape, and Post-it notes, just to name a few. Canon's core competency is optics. Motorola's is wireless communications, and Boeing's is aircraft. Any new products you see coming from these companies will probably be new applications of what they do well.

Similarly, your best chance for creative success will come from building on those things you know about and have experience in. The obvious lesson here is *know thyself.* Trying to get innovative in areas you know little or nothing about is usually a money-losing proposition.

For example, my core competency is creating and communicating business information that helps people work smarter. Consequently, any new products or services I develop are based on that core competency. Barring some very unforeseen happenings, you aren't likely to find me writing books with titles such as "Total Breathing," "The Cat Who Was Embraced by the Light in Madison County," or "Men Who Love Sheep and Women Who Won't Wear Wool."

Your Best Creative Partner Is Your Customer

Have you ever wondered where most ideas for new products originate? It isn't in the research labs of big corporations or universities, according to Eric von Hippel of the Massachusetts Institute of Technology. In his research, von Hippel found that approximately 80 percent of all new product ideas are initiated by the customer in an attempt to solve a problem. Once again, we have an obvious but often overlooked strategy for successful innovation: *Know thy customer.* Your best sources for new ideas are your customers and those whom you want to become your customers.

You aren't going to find great new ideas for your business by locking yourself in your home office and thinking. You may come up with a great idea while doing that, but it takes more. You need to know your customers' unmet wants and needs and apply your unique strengths to solve their problems. How do you find their unmet wants? Obviously, asking them is a good starting point. Simply listening to your customers and giving them what they want can be extremely profitable. But the best ideas will probably come from staying close to your customers and working directly with them.

Think of your customers as creative partners. Spend some time visiting with them. Ask if you can observe or work with them as they use what they buy from you. If you're developing a new product or service, include your customers in the design process. Ask them for ideas and let them try out those ideas to see what they like and don't like. Use their ideas to refine your new product or service to make it more valuable to them. The more you know about your customers and their problems, the more likely you are to come up with very profitable ideas.

Create an Innovative Climate

One of the great things about being a micropreneur is that you have to motivate only yourself. Consequently, it's your job—and well within your ability—to create a climate that will encourage and motivate you to come up with new ideas. Here are some ways that will help:

1. Establish an incentive at the outset. In short, what's in it for you? More money? Less time-consuming work? A better career? Personal satisfaction? The best ideas come from those who know what they want and have a burning desire to achieve it.

Even after Thomas Edison became wealthy, his main motivation for inventing was money. As he put it, "Anything that won't sell, I don't want to invent." While that may seem terribly mercenary, it makes a lot of sense from an altruistic viewpoint. Any new product or service that millions of people are willing to pay for will probably benefit them and make the world a better place. Edison's genius was worth infinitely more to mankind than the amount of money he earned in his lifetime. That's the beauty of private enterprise. You can get rich by helping others and making the world a better place.

2. Use the 15/15 rule. Thinking up and trying out new business ideas takes time and money—two of your most precious resources. If you wait until you have enough of each, you may wait forever. On the other hand, spending too much time and money on new ideas is a great way to go broke.

That's where the 15/15 rule comes in. Allocate 15 percent of your time and 15 percent of your gross revenues to experiment with new ways to make or save money. That way, you're investing some of your resources in new ideas without betting the company store.

The 3M Corporation, one of the world's most innovative companies, allows any employee to spend up to 15 percent of the workweek doing whatever he or she wants as long as it's product-related. One of the many profitable ideas to come from this practice was the invention of Post-it notes and products, which earn 3M hundreds of millions of dollars each year.

3. Give yourself the right to be wrong. Innovation is a numbers game and the odds of any one idea being a grand-slam home run are small. But you aren't going to hit a grand slam unless you keep stepping up to the plate. When ideas don't work—and many of them won't—consider it as part of the price you pay for future success and learn from it. If you keep trying and learning, you'll eventually hit a big money-maker that will compensate many times over for all the money-losers. An innovative disappointment can be a springboard to future success, if you're smart enough to learn from it. I don't believe in success and failure. I believe in success and learning.

4. Relax and have fun with your ideas. Rigid, structured, serious thinking and behavior is one sure way to kill creativity. That's why so many big corporations and organizations find themselves devoid of fresh ideas. They tell people how to dress, when to come to work, how to do the job, how to behave, and when to go home. Then they wonder why the company lacks imagination.

Years ago, T. H. Huxley wrote, "The secret of genius is to carry the spirit of childhood into maturity." Creativity flourishes best in an environment where there's a relaxed spirit of playfulness. Being able to relax as you think stimulates creativity. So don't make the mistake of trying to be serious and creative at the same time. Let your mind wander. Use your sense of humor. Avoid being too careful. Think of creative thinking as fun and you're more likely to come up with some seriously profitable ideas.

5. Create opportunities for both interaction and solitude. Good business ideas don't originate in a vacuum. The more you interact and learn from other people, the more ideas you'll produce. Make it your business to meet regularly with others. Customers, friends, family, and other micropreneurs can provide you with the information, stimulation, and feedback you need to create new solutions to your problems or refine any new ideas you have. The key is to choose those who are positive, creative, and supportive. As Walt Disney remarked, "Most of my good ideas come from others. That's because whenever I spot an idea that I think my friends can use, I pass it along. They in turn do the same thing for me. It works like magic."

While interaction is necessary, it's also important to realize that every new idea is the product of a single brain. You also need time alone to think ideas through. Solitary creative thinking works best when you carve out large blocks of time to concentrate on the problem at hand. When you're looking for ways to solve a problem, give yourself at least 90 minutes, preferably two or more hours, to concentrate on it. Research on creativity conducted by Donald McKinnon, a psychologist at the University of California, Berkeley, revealed that those people who spent more time pondering a problem were likely to have the most creative solutions.

6. Finally, believe in your creative powers and you'll get the ideas you want. Once again, we become what we think about. Believe you're creative, and your subconscious will create the reality. As comedian John Cleese put it, "This is the extraordinary thing about creativity: If you just keep your mind around the subject in a friendly but persistent

way, . . . sooner or later you will get a reward from your unconscious."

HOW TO CREATE AND FIND GREAT NEW IDEAS

In addition to creating a creative climate, you can also improve your ability to think up and discover great new ideas with the application of a few simple techniques. Here are the ones I find most useful:

Use the Creative Problem-solving Process

Students and practitioners of creative thinking have found that the process of creating good new ideas goes through a somewhat predictable cycle. For purposes of simplicity, the process can be divided into five steps. Use the following five steps the next time you're searching for answers to a problem:

1. *First Insight.* According to Thomas Edison, "Restless discontents are the first necessities of progress." The creative process starts at the moment you discover and begin to focus on a problem you want solved or an activity you want to do. You want to quit your job and work from home. You like working from home but don't like the business you're in and want to do something else. You want to double your business without increasing your overhead. You need to find new customers or keep more of the ones you already have. These are all examples of first insight. Put another way, you're defining a problem. Generating the right ideas to solve the problem may be months or years away, but this first step is essential. Never underestimate the value of luck, but luck happens to people who know what they're looking for.

2. *Preparation.* With a problem well defined, the next step is to do your homework and investigate as many ways as

possible to solve the problem or expand the idea. Read. Observe. Take notes. Talk to others. Ask questions and collect as much information as you can about the subject. The more ideas you can collect about a subject, the better. We come up with the best new ideas after we thoroughly familiarize ourselves with the ideas of others. This is the hardest and most time-consuming part of the process, but it's an essential one. The best ideas come to those who do their homework.

3. *Incubation.* After a lengthy amount of preparation, you may feel frustrated, be suffering from information overload, and think that you're making no progress. But that's usually not the case. It's just part of the process. When that happens, the next step is to turn the problem over to your subconscious. Don't work on the problem or worry about it. Sleep on it. Take a walk. Take a vacation. Let your thoughts go underground. Our most important decisions are made at the subconscious level.

This period of incubation may be long or short, but it has to occur. The novelist Edna Ferber said, "A story must simmer in its own juice for months or years before it's ready to serve." Whether it takes minutes, months, or years, creative thinking requires that you give your subconscious time to work.

4. *Illumination.* This is the euphoric stage of the creative process, when your subconscious suddenly delivers a seemingly great new idea to your conscious mind. Eureka! That's it! That's what I'm going to do! Great new ideas come at the least-expected times and seem to appear out of nowhere. But the truly good insights usually occur after an extensive amount of preparation and incubation. Archimedes got the insight for his law while bathing. Similarly, Charles Darwin's theory came to him while riding in a carriage. And Isaac Newton was sitting under a tree when an apple fell on him. But all three men received their creative insights after years of studying the problem.

5. *Verification.* Once you get a new idea, you need to evaluate it objectively to determine if it's any good. Like it or not, the creative process will generate a lot of new ideas, and most of them are worthless. Back off from your idea and look at it as objectively as possible. If it's an idea for a new product or service, ask your customers what they think about it. Get as much candid and objective feedback as you can. Ask for ways to refine or improve on the idea to make it even better.

The next time you're wrestling with a major problem and trying to solve it, use this process and you'll find it very worthwhile. First, define the problem and write it down. Then, do your homework and gather as much information as you can. When you feel saturated with information, forget the problem and let your subconscious work on it. Sooner or later, you'll have new ideas seemingly coming out of nowhere. Check them out. You may have a few diamonds in the rough.

Question the Status Quo and Challenge Assumptions

When you're trying to do better things and do things better, be a questioner. Take a product, service, or anything you're trying to improve and ask a series of questions about it. Here's a list of questions to help get your mind going:

- Is there a new way to do it?
- Can you make it bigger or smaller?
- Can you add something to it, subtract something from it, or rearrange the order of things?
- Can you combine this with something?
- What if you do the opposite of this?
- Can something be substituted?
- How can you make it better, faster, or cheaper?
- What else can be adapted?
- What if you don't do anything?
- How can you give this a new twist?
- What else can you use this for?

- Who else has use for this?
- How can you make this more salable?

Questions are the creative acts of intelligence, and asking the right questions often causes your imagination to come up with just the right new idea. Like processionary caterpillars, most people don't question why things are the way they are. They just assume someone else has all the right answers and blindly follow. But creative types are forever questioning the way things are in the hope of finding a new insight or a better way to do things. Everyone believed that the world was the center of the universe until Copernicus challenged the idea and came up with evidence to the contrary.

Be a Creative Borrower

Always be on the lookout for great ideas that you can adapt to your business. Sam Walton visited Sol Price's Price CostCo and borrowed the idea to create Sam's Wholesale Club. George Thomas borrowed an idea from a ballpoint pen and created the roll-on deodorant applicator. Ford borrowed the best ideas of numerous makes and models of cars from all over the world and created the Ford Taurus and Mercury Sable. All are examples of creative borrowing.

Creative borrowing can be very profitable, but it's important to realize that certain types of borrowing are off-limits and can get you in trouble. Borrowing an idea is fine, as long as it's not patented, copyrighted, or trademarked and taken verbatim. For example, it's okay for Sam Walton to start a discount club. But he can't use Price's logos, packaging, brand name, advertising, and the like. If you have doubts about the legality of borrowing an idea from someone, ask for his permission or run it by an attorney who is knowledgeable in the area of patents, trademarks, and copyrights. But make it a goal to find at least one new idea each day that you can borrow to grow your business. It's a habit that will repay you many times over.

Get a New Frame of Reference

Creativity is the ability to make new things familiar and familiar things new. It's been said that if you can look at something and see only what everyone else sees, you are so much a product of your culture that you're a victim of it. The best new ideas often come when you look at something from a different viewpoint. Trying to see your business from your customer's frame of reference instead of your own is one example. As the 19th-century psychologist William James said, "Genius, in truth, means little more than the faculty of perceiving in an unhabitual way." The following quotes illustrate perceiving subjects in unhabitual ways:

From the hayloft, a horse looks like a violin.
—LORD CHESTERFIELD

A hen is only an egg's way of making another egg.
—SAMUEL BUTLER

Man—a creature made at the end of the week's work when God was tired.
—MARK TWAIN

Xerox: a trade name that can make rapid reproductions of human error perfectly.
—MERLE L. MEACHAM

One of the hot topics in business today is the need to see the world through a new paradigm. The underlying message is that technology has changed the world and the rules for success. If you try to succeed with an outdated view of the world, your business and economic future are in jeopardy. The future is brightest for those who can view the world with a fresh pair of eyes and see it from different perspectives.

Years ago, Napoleon said to inventor Robert Fulton,

"What, sir, you would make a ship sail against the wind and currents by lighting a bonfire under her decks? I pray you excuse me. I have no time to listen to such nonsense." We can only wonder how different history might have been had Napoleon listened with a fresh perspective and an open mind.

Capture and Bank Your Ideas

Always have something nearby to record your thoughts or observations. There is absolutely no way to predict when a great new idea is going to walk into your life, and it's been my experience that they come at the least-expected times. Ideas are thoughts, and thoughts are soon forgotten unless you have some way to record them permanently. The philosopher Eric Hoffer wrote, "That which is unique and worthwhile in us makes itself felt only in flashes. If we do not know how to catch and savor these flashes, we are without growth and exhilaration."

Make it a habit to carry a pen and something to jot down ideas on. If you prefer to use a microcassette recorder or a pocket electronic organizer or pocket-size photocopier to record your ideas, that's fine. Just don't go *anywhere* without a way to record your ideas. Whenever I travel, I always carry a pair of scissors to clip items of interest from newspapers and magazines. If you want something more expensive and sophisticated, there are on-line clipping services. For a fee, they will forward articles to you on the subject of your choice via your computer. It's also a good idea to bring a camera. Remember all those Japanese businessmen who toured U.S. plants with cameras around their necks? They weren't taking pictures just for fun.

Once you begin collecting ideas, store them in an idea file or several idea files based on subject matter. Those are the seeds of your new, moneymaking ideas. For example, let's say you have a folder of potential new product or service ideas that you have been collecting. When you want to create a new product or service, open your idea file and pick up two or three of the items in it. Can any of these be combined, rearranged, or added to something else to create a new moneymaker for you? Soon you'll find yourself creating a lot of new moneymaking ideas. As David Greenberg remarked, "Life is like a kaleidoscope. You have all the pieces you need to make great designs."

The essence of creativity is modifying and making connections between previously unrelated concepts or things. Clarence Birdseye went to Canada and ate some fish that had been frozen and thawed naturally. He related the idea to food sales, and the frozen-food industry was born. The French physician René Laënnec remembered how he signaled to his friends on a hollow log as a child. From this idea, he invented the stethoscope. Ben Franklin got tired of changing eyeglasses and invented bifocal lenses.

Be Ready to Pounce on the Unexpected

It's called serendipity, the knack of making unexpected and accidental discoveries. Ideas and opportunities are all around us, and it's our job to recognize and capitalize on them. My favorite definition of luck is "opportunity meeting preparation." Here are some well-known examples of serendipity in action:

• A chemist dropped on the floor a flask containing a liquid plastic substance. When he picked up the pieces, he noticed they stuck together. The result of this accident was the invention of shatterproof glass.

• When Alexander Fleming was examining culture plates contaminated by mold under a microscope, he saw islands of bacteria surrounded by clear spaces. He wondered if the mold could be preventing the spread of bacteria. The mold was *Penicillium notatum,* and it formed an antibiotic that was named penicillin. Thus, the era of antibiotics was born.

- A group of 3M researchers were trying to develop a synthetic rubber for jet-aircraft hoses. A beaker containing some of the trial substance fell on a lab technician's tennis shoe, and no standard cleaning solvent could remove it. With further refinement, the substance became Scotchgard fabric protector.

- Clarence Crane, a chocolate dealer, sold peppermints during the summer, when chocolate sales declined. He had the mints pressed into shape by a local pill manufacturer. In 1912 the machine malfunctioned and pressed out peppermint rings instead of solid mints. Instead of complaining about deformed mints, Crane knew he had a unique product, which he called Life Savers. That was many billions of rolls ago.

Many a fortune has been started from home due to an unforeseen, unpleasant, or unexpected occurrence. Here are several examples:

- Bette Nesmith, in the hope of saving her job as a bank secretary, covered her typos with a mixture of water-based paint and a coloring agent that blended perfectly with the bank's stationery. It worked so well that she started bottling and selling it out of her garage. Years later, the Gillette Company bought Nesmith's Liquid Paper Corporation for $47.5 million.

- Stephen Wozniak asked on three different occasions if he could help work on the personal computer his employer was designing, and was turned down each time. So he went home, created his own computer, called it the Apple, and subsequently formed Apple Computer with Steven Jobs.

- In 1951 Lillian Vernon, expecting her first child and seeking a way to make money from home, placed a $495 advertisement in *Seventeen* magazine for belts and purses. In the ad, she offered to personalize orders with each customers' initials at no additional cost. From that one ad, she received $32,000 worth of orders and launched one of the most successful catalog-sales companies of our time.

If you look back on your own life, some of your greatest fortunes have, no doubt, been accidental and initially unpleasant. Always look for unexpected opportunities and be ready to act on them. Did you just lose your job? Here's your opportunity to start your own business at home. One key to living a successfully creative life lies in turning unpleasant or accidental experiences into something positive.

Create Now, Judge Later

It's been said that the mind, like a parachute, works best when opened. One sure way to curtail your ability to think up ideas is to try to think up and judge them at the same time. When you're thinking up ideas, suspend all judgment. Go for quantity. Write all of them down. Then, after you have exhausted your idea-generating capability, go back and choose the best ones for further study and implementation. The late Dr. Linus Pauling said it best: "To have a good idea, you have to have lots of ideas."

Finally, here are some thoughts to help with a very important question:

How Can You Tell if You Have a Good Idea?

The honest answer is, "I don't know." Neither does anyone else. There is no surefire way to tell if your seemingly wonderful new idea is a big winner unless you invest some time, effort, and money in it. But you can improve the odds of success by testing your idea against some important criteria. If the idea doesn't pass those criteria, forget it. If it does, try testing it out on a small scale if possible. Judge the value of an idea by emotionally distancing yourself from it and answering the following questions:

1. *Will it work?* In short, will it get the results you want? Will it do what you want it to do? Will it solve the problem? Will it provide the customer with benefits he or she will buy? If it's a moneymaking idea, will it make money? If it's a money-saving idea, will it save money? Most ideas won't pass this first crucial test, but that doesn't necessarily mean the idea should be abandoned. Perhaps it can be refined or modified to make it work. It took Edison over 6,000 tries before he came up with a workable filament for the electric light bulb. If he had given up on the first try, we might all still be reading by candlelight.

2. *Is it better than what already exists?* There is no sense in replacing the wheel with the runner. Have you come up with a new idea where much is to be gained by changing to it? People aren't going to change just because you want them to. Unless your innovation is significantly better than the one it's designed to replace, there's no incentive for you or anyone else to adopt it.

3. *Is it user-friendly?* If people have to modify or make uncomfortable changes in their behavior, chances for success are slim to none. There must be an enormous benefit to offset any user discomfort, or the idea will never fly.

4. *How badly do you want to try this idea?* That question is important only when you have to make a major investment of time, money, and energy. For example, how badly do you want to succeed in your own home-based business? Are you willing to commit yourself to doing whatever it takes to make it work? Behind every successful big idea that works is usually someone who has the desire and determination to make it work.

5. *Is the timing right?* There's no such thing as the right idea at the wrong time. Look at the trends. Is your idea in step with the times? Are you too far ahead of the time? Is this an idea whose time has come and gone? The best ideas are, to paraphrase Panasonic, just slightly ahead of their time. The pioneers get the arrows and those who are late to the party get the leftovers. Those just slightly ahead of their time get the money.

6. *Is it worth it?* Some ideas cost more to implement than the benefits they deliver. If it's a new product or service, will what it does for customers be worth more to them than the money they have to pay for it? If it's a better way to get things done, will it save you more in time, effort, and money than the cost of implementing it? Like everything else in business, ideas have to deliver perceived value to be valuable.

If your new idea scores a resounding yes on all six questions, you probably have a good one worth pursuing. But before pouring your heart and soul into it, check it out with someone who is knowledgeable about the subject, can be objective, and can give you some honest feedback. And give yourself some time to get away from the idea and let it cool. That way, you can view it from a more detached perspective. The key to a great future is to create it. And the way to create it is by using your time to turn great ideas into successful realities.

8

How to Turn Time into Money

When you do the things you *need* to do when you
ought to do them, the day will come when you can do
the things you *want* to do when you *want* to do them.

—DR. ROBERT ANTHONY

A man moved to a new city and went looking for a church to
join. He visited several churches and was having a hard time
finding one where he felt comfortable. Just when he was
about to give up, he passed by a church, looked in, and heard
the preacher say, "We have left undone those things which
we ought to have done. And we have done those things which
we ought not to have done." The newcomer immediately settled into a pew and, with a deep sigh of relief, said to himself,
Thank God! I've found my crowd at last.

One of the most important things you need to know as a
micropreneur is this: Regardless of your product and/or service, *what you're really selling is your time.* The truth is that we all
sell our time in the marketplace. But most people don't realize that time is money and practically give it away. There's a
lot of truth to the old axiom, "I bargained my life for a penny
and life paid not a penny more."

Businesses are fond of calculating and paying close attention to their ROI, or return on investment. If you're going to be successful in your one-person business, you need to pay close attention to your ROTE—return on time and energy. Those are your only real resources, and you can't afford to squander them. Time is your most precious resource and a raw material of everything you produce.

It's common to hear about how hard the self-employed work and what long hours they put in. While I work long hours at times, I'm sure at least half the working population puts in a lot more hours than I do. It's not because I'm so smart. It's because I know what I want to accomplish when I sit down to work, and I make good use of my time. But there are a few simple ideas and techniques that anyone can use.

Time-management systems are like diets. Every year someone claims to have discovered a whole new system that will make quantum-leap improvements in your performance. In truth, good time-management principles and practices have been around for years. Like diets, just about any time-management system works if you're well focused, know what you're trying to accomplish, and stick with it.

The term *time management* is a real misnomer, because time is totally unmanageable. It's a resource constantly being depleted at a predictable rate—60 minutes an hour, 24 hours a day, 365 days a year. All we can do is manage ourselves in a way that will make effective use of time. But before you start learning and practicing time-management techniques, you should understand two very important distinctions if you want to take a lot of stress out of your life and put more productivity, satisfaction, and freedom into it.

1. Distinguish Between Efficiency and Effectiveness.

Efficiency is doing a job right. Effectiveness is doing the right job. Effectiveness is measured by results, and when you're a micropreneur, results are everything.

All too often, people who want to make better use of their time begin by trying to do what they're currently doing more efficiently. That may or may not be a good idea, but it's the wrong starting point. It makes little or no difference how efficiently you manage your time if you aren't spending it pursuing the results you need to achieve. Do the right job inefficiently, and your business will survive. Do the wrong job efficiently and you go broke. Do the right job efficiently and someday you'll be set for life. Efficiency is only valuable when it contributes to effectiveness.

2. Distinguish Between Urgency and Importance.

The longer I live, the more I'm convinced that the ability to distinguish between urgency and importance is crucial to working and living successfully. And the inability to distinguish between the two gets us in trouble and ultimately results in shattered dreams and a wasted life.

Every day we have things that happen and things to do. Some of them are urgent. Some are important. Some are both. Some are neither. Here's what you need to remember: *Urgent things are seldom important, and important things are seldom urgent.* Unfortunately, most of us spend the bulk of our lives responding to the urgent as if everything that's urgent is important.

Driving frantically to get to a meeting on time is urgent. Getting there safely is important. Finishing a project on time is urgent. Doing a quality job is important. Working long hours to get your business off the ground is urgent. Making time to exercise, eat properly, and get enough rest is important. Closing the sale is urgent. Building a business based on customer satisfaction and repeat business is important. Having a flashy new car or an expensive new dress is urgent. Saving and investing to become financially independent is important.

If you spend your time responding to the tyranny of the urgent, your life is going to be far less successful than it could be. That's one reason why so many people today are working harder, living poorer, and feeling so time starved. They allow urgent things to dictate how their time is spent and important things to go neglected. And you can imagine what happens when important things are neglected. Sooner or later, they become urgent *and* important. They're called crises. Money crises. Health crises. Business crises. Family crises. Most of them are preventable if we choose to spend our time doing what's important instead of responding to what's urgent.

Because you are the sum of your choices, one of the most important choices you can make is to decide what's important. Then commit yourself to spending your time achieving important results rather than responding to urgent and unimportant distractions.

TURNING TIME INTO MONEY IS AS SIMPLE AS 1-2-3

Time-management systems may be simple or complex, but they all evolve around three basic steps:

1. Decide What's Important.

If you've taken the time to create mission and vision statements, you have already completed this step. Your mission and vision statements tell you what's most important. Put another way, their purpose is to remind you of the values your business is built on. When you spend the bulk of your time doing work that's in line with those values, you'll find yourself turning time into money and enjoying the process. That's why it's vital that you have a well-defined mission and vision for your business.

If you haven't written mission and vision statements for your business, do it now. Once you have a clear picture of how you plan to create value for your customers and where you want your business to take you, you have a strategy for turning time into money.

2. Set Goals and Priorities to Do What's Important.

Your next step is to put that strategy into action. To do that, you need to set specific goals and priorities. Without them, you'll waste your time with activities that get you nowhere. But once you decide on the results you want to achieve, you know where to invest the bulk of your time and you'll be working effectively.

3. Develop Good Work Habits.

Your final step is to achieve your goals with the minimum investment of time and energy—in other words, to work efficiently. In summary, then, good time management is:

- deciding what's most important,
- setting goals and priorities to do what's most important, and
- developing good work habits to do the most important things in the most efficient way.

SETTING GOALS AND PRIORITIES

Your mission and vision statements should give you a general picture of what you want to achieve. But now you have to get down to particulars by setting specific goals. Here are some important guidelines you need to know about setting goals:

1. Set your own goals. It's your business, your career, and your life. Take charge of it and do what's meaningful and best for you. Getting the advice and counsel of friends, family, experts, and others is wise, but the success of your business is ultimately up to you. Therefore, you and only you should make the final decisions about what your goals will be.

2. Put your goals in writing. If it's important enough to be a goal, it should be written down. Writing goals increases clarity and commitment.

3. Your goals should be challenging but attainable. When a goal seems impossible, we give up too easily. When it's too easy, we get bored. A worthwhile goal is the one you can achieve by pushing yourself to perform a little bit better than you have in the past.

4. Every goal should have a deadline. If it doesn't have a target date for completion, it's not a goal. It's a daydream. Dreaming is fine in its place, but it's not setting a goal.

5. Major goals should be measurable. You need a way to keep score to see if you're getting the results you want. For example:

- Dollars of sales per month
- Number of units produced per week
- Number of sales calls made per week
- Percentage of sales closed
- Monthly overhead in dollars or as a percentage of revenue
- Percentage of sales coming from repeat customers

Every major goal should have a performance indicator and the criteria for success at the outset. If you can't measure or describe what you want to achieve, it isn't clear enough in your own mind to be a goal.

6. Your goals should be compatible with each other and with your mission and vision statements. If you want to attend an important conference and buy a new computer this year but can't afford both, you have incompatible goals. Your goals should work in harmony toward the ultimate goal of making you set for life.

7. Setting priorities for your goals is essential. Some goals are more important than others. Some you must do. Some you should do. Some are nice to do. Rank your goals in order of importance and make sure you achieve the most important ones. Good time management means doing important things first.

Getting Started

Turning time into money begins with investing a nice chunk of time into some thoughtful planning. It's generally agreed that every hour of sound planning saves three or four hours in execution. And like your goals, your plans should be written down. So set aside some time to do your thinking on paper.

As a micropreneur, you're the CEO of the marketing, production, finance, and research departments, and you have to perform well in all four areas. Here are some questions whose answers will help you set some start-up goals for each area. Write your answers down on paper.

Marketing: Who are your potential customers? How are you going to attract their attention and get them to buy from you? How much revenue will you bring in for the first six months? The first year?

Production: What's your basic product and/or service? What tools do you need to be productive? When can you have a salable product on the market?

Finance: How much is it going to cost to get the business up and running? How long will it take to recover the set-up costs? What percentage of gross profit on sales do you expect? How will you keep your operating expenses low? What is the maximum amount you're willing to invest in the business in the first year?

Research: What should you be learning to become excellent at this business? Whom should you talk to? What books should you read? What organizations should you join?

When you finish answering these questions, write down at

least one measurable goal for marketing, production, finance, and research that you will achieve in the next 6 months, the next 12 months, or whatever time frame you deem appropriate. These are your Start-up Goals. If you have several goals in each category, rank them in order of importance.

Choose one goal from all four categories that you must achieve and write each down. These are your Most Important Goals, the ones you need to focus on every day until you achieve them. When you achieve all of your most important goals, go back to your Start-up Goals list, choose the next most important goals in each category, and move them to your Most Important Goals list. At the end of whatever time period you have chosen, measure your performance against each of your Start-up Goals and set marketing, production, finance, and research goals for the next period.

Make a Daily Things-to-Do List

When you go to work each day, have your Most Important Goals list on your desk or someplace where it will remind you of the results you're working to achieve. Then start each day by making a list of Things to Do that day that will move you closer to achieving one or more of your most important goals.

You may find it helps to categorize the items on your Things-to-Do list in order of their importance. The A items you must do. The B items you should do. The C items would be nice to do. Then you number the goals in each category. And when you go to work each day, start with the As, not the Cs. Don't worry if you don't complete the list. If you can't get everything done with this system, you'll get the most important things done.

The concept of setting goals and priorities and making a daily Things-to-Do list is centuries old. Yet it remains a highly popular time-management system for two reasons. It's simple and it works.

The reason it works is best explained by a principle known as Pareto's law, or, more popularly, the 80/20 rule. Basically the 80/20 rule states that 80 percent of the value of a group of items is generally concentrated in only 20 percent of those items. For example, 80 percent of your sales will probably come from 20 percent of your customers. Eighty percent of your telephone calls will come from 20 percent of your callers. And *80 percent of your effectiveness will come from achieving 20 percent of your goals.* That's why it's essential that the bulk of your working time be spent pursuing your most important goals and the most important items on your Things-to-Do list.

Making First-rate Habits Second Nature

When you set goals and priorities and work on achieving the most important goals, you're focused on getting results. You've taken a giant step toward turning time into money. Your next task is to learn how to turn time into money efficiently. The more efficient you become, the more money you'll get for your time, and the sooner you'll be financially independent.

Here's a very important fact about time usage. We tend to spend most of our time in recurring patterns of behavior without giving much thought to them. Some of these habits are time-savers while others waste copious amounts of time. The key to becoming efficient at time usage is to identify the time-wasting habits and replace them with ones that will help you turn time into money. Here's how to do that:

1. Find Out How You're Spending Your Time.

Keep a time log for a week. Write down every work activity you engage in and how long it takes. At the end of the week, add up how much time you spent in each of your work activities. For example, how much time did you spend on the telephone, in face-to-face contact with customers, traveling, attending meetings, dealing with interruptions, learning new skills, reading, paperwork, and at lunch?

Finding out how your time is actually being spent is usually a real eye-opener. We don't realize the huge amount of time we waste on needless activities that don't contribute to achieving our goals. Most of us waste about half our time, and the best of us waste a good two hours each day.

Once you have completed a time-log exercise for your working week, write down the answers to the following questions:

- What are my three greatest time-wasters?
- How much time is being consumed by needless interruptions? Who or what is most responsible for them? How can they be minimized?
- What am I doing that's urgent but unimportant? How can these activities be reduced or eliminated?
- What are my most- and least-productive times of the day?
- Whom do I need to spend more time with? Whom do I need to see less of?
- What activities should I be devoting more time to?
- What activities should I be spending less time on?
- What activities can be eliminated or delegated?
- Am I trying to do too much?
- Am I procrastinating?
- What habits or tendencies are causing me to waste time?

2. Choose New Habits to Replace Old Ones.

If you know your goals and priorities and have written answers to the questions about how you should spend your time each working day, you will have plenty of good ideas for getting more done in less time. All it takes is the willingness to replace time-wasting habits with productive ones.

Some years ago I assembled a list of 12 of the most common time wasters that plague all of us. Accompanying each time waster is a good new habit to speed up your work.

Time Waster	New Habit
1. Failure to get the most important things done.	Look at your daily Things-to-Do list. Then try to schedule your day to work on the most important tasks during prime time, the time of day when your energy is highest. That way, you give your best self to the most important tasks.
2. Paper shuffling	Try to handle each piece of paper only once. Every time you pick up a piece of paper, throw it away, file it, or do something to move it on its way.
3. Cluttered desk	Clear the top of your desk of everything except the item you're working on. If this isn't practical, resolve to clear your desk at the end of each workday. Don't let reading material build up. Read it by a certain date or throw it away.
4. Routine and trivia	Save routine and trivial items and do them in batches in non-prime time when your energy level is low.
5. Trying to do too much	Don't do anything unnecessary. Practice saying no politely and rapidly. Slow down. The key to doing more is to do less better.
6. Afternoon drowsiness	Eat a light lunch.

7. Too many interruptions	Establish a quiet time each day during which you can work undisturbed.
8. Drop-in visitors	Establish working hours and let those who drop in know what they are. Close your office door. Don't answer the doorbell. Schedule breaks and lunch hours to see those you need to see.
9. The telephone	Have calls screened or use voice mail to take incoming messages. Establish a time for placing and receiving calls. Put a three-minute hourglass by your telephone and try to complete calls in three minutes or less.
10. Meetings	Never go if you can avoid it. Get off boards and committees. If you're in charge, schedule starting and ending times and stick to the schedule. Schedule meetings at lunch or at the end of the day to prevent them from dragging on.
11. Indecision	Accept risks as inevitable. Gather information, give yourself a deadline, and make a choice. People who are afraid to make decisions end up working for those who do.
12. Procrastination	Break up that overwhelming job you're putting off into as many small jobs as you can. Give yourself a deadline for

completing the entire project
and work on it a little bit every
day, starting today. Write the
words "Do it now!" and post
them where you work.

3. Replace the Old Habits with New Ones.

Making first-rate habits second nature is much easier said
than done. New habits don't feel comfortable at first, and you
have to muster the willpower to practice them until they do.
As runner Jim Ryan remarked, "Motivation is what gets you
started. Habit is what keeps you going."

A good way to get started is to choose only one new habit
and practice it without fail for three weeks. It normally takes
three weeks for a new habit to feel comfortable. Once you're
comfortable with the new habit, choose another and practice
it for three weeks. Then choose another, and so on. Soon
you'll find yourself getting a lot more done with a lot less
stress. It's also very important that you begin immediately. If
you wait until you feel inspired, you'll wait forever. Just act the
way you want to be and soon you'll be the way you act.

How do you motivate yourself to adopt and practice good
work habits? One way is to give yourself a reward for practicing a new habit unfailingly for three weeks. It can be anything you want—a special meal at a nice restaurant, a
weekend vacation, or a special play or sporting event. If you
practice the habit for three straight weeks, give yourself the
reward. Just be sure to be honest with yourself.

If you have trouble keeping commitments to yourself,
make them to someone else. Bet your spouse or a friend that
you'll either achieve your most important goals or buy them
a dinner at the restaurant of their choice. And think about
how someday all these new habits are going to help make you
set for life. Every new good habit you acquire comes with the
built-in benefits of higher productivity, less stress, and more
time to do what you want. You're acquiring the skills that turn

raw talent into profitable ability. In the long run, the entire payoff is to you.

4. Be Disciplined but Flexible.

A final word of caution: Don't become a time nut. Practicing any of these strategies and techniques in a rigid, mechanistic fashion is a blueprint for insanity and will be counterproductive. Don't rigidly over-schedule your day with activities, because no day will go as planned. Running around with a stopwatch and being compulsive about keeping a clear desk isn't going to make you more productive. It's a good practice to schedule quiet time to work alone. But common sense dictates that important customers and valued partners who need to see you or speak with you on the telephone will take precedence.

None of us can do everything efficiently all of the time, and life would be pretty dull if we could. But all of us can practice good time-management habits some of the time if we are aware of them and apply them with a healthy dose of flexibility and common sense. That's why having goals and priorities is so important. When you know what you're trying to accomplish, you can ask yourself, What's the best use of my time and energy right now? and the answer is usually obvious. Then you apply self-discipline and the right work habits to make the best use of your time and energy. It's sometimes uncomfortable in the short run but much easier in the long run.

In summary, the key to turning time into money is simply having a well-thought-out major plan and the self-discipline to work at it every day. It's doing your best work even when you don't feel like it, because you realize that *now* is the most important time. Why? Because now is the only time over which you have any control.

9

Multiply Yourself with Smart Tools

Technology is like a steamroller. If you're not on the
steamroller, then you are destined to become part of
the road.

—*BITS & PIECES* MAGAZINE

A Japanese man and a Texan were passing through customs
at an airport. The Japanese man had two large suitcases, and
the Texan was helping him move them toward the customs
officer when the Japanese man's wristwatch started to beep.
He listened to the message and talked through a miniature
speaker on the telephone in the watch. The Texan was
amazed and offered the man $5,000 for his watch. "The
watch is not for sale," he replied.

The Texan continued to help the Japanese man push his
heavy bags forward, and a few seconds later the watch
beeped again. This time the man opened the watch to receive an E-mail message on a small screen and used the small
computer contained in the watch to reply to the message.
The Texan watched in awe and offered him $25,000 for the
watch. Again he was told, "The watch is not for sale." And
again the Texan helped push the enormous bags forward.

The watch beeped a third time, and this time a long fax

came out. The Texan, determined to have the watch, upped his offer to $300,000. The Japanese man asked if he had the money, and the Texan wrote him a check on the spot. The Japanese man processed the check on his watch and transferred the money into his Swiss bank account. He took off the watch, handed it to the Texan, and walked away.

"Wait!" the Texan called out. "You're forgetting your bags."

"Those aren't my bags," the Japanese man shouted back. "They're the batteries for your watch!"

Oh, the joys of the information age. Modern communications technology, more than anything else, is what's enabling so many of us to make our fortunes working at home or anywhere else we want. Computers, cellular phones, voice mail, fax machines, beepers, telecommunications, and all the wonderful tools of the information age have enabled us to transcend time and space. As the young actress Anna Paquin remarks in a popular long-distance-telephone company commercial, "There is no there. We are all here."

WELCOME TO THE AGE OF VIRTUAL STUPIDITY

Have you noticed how frequently the word "virtual" appears in descriptions of topics relevant to the information age? We read and hear about:

- Virtual organizations and teams that are rapidly created to do a job and are dissolved just as quickly when the job is done.
- Virtual offices (consisting of laptop computers, cellular phones, personal digital assistants, and the like) that allow us to transact business and do our jobs at the speed of light from anywhere on earth.
- Virtual reality where we put on goggles and earphones and experience an exciting adventure or happening as if we were actually there.

I would like to add a new term to your "virtual" vocabulary: *virtual stupidity*. It's the unintentional practice of becoming so engrossed and mesmerized by the tools of information technology that you forget the reason you bought them in the first place—to leverage your time and grow your business.

Information technology, like the human mind, is a two-edged sword. Properly used, these tools can make you rich by multiplying your value and productivity. But these same tools will suck the time out of your life and add needless overhead to your business if you allow them to. It's one key reason why many of us are so time starved. We take the gadgets wherever we go and never leave the office behind. We spend copious amounts of time learning all the things our personal computer can do instead of learning the few skills we need to make us more productive and ignoring the rest. We spend time playing computer games and chatting with friends on-line instead of doing what needs to be done. Rather than mastering the tools of information technology, we become their slaves.

The antidote for virtual stupidity is the simplicity rule: *If it doesn't add value, don't do it.* Don't invest your time and money in buying or learning how to use anything unless you clearly understand how the payoff will be worth far more to you than the cost. Every piece of computer hardware and software, telephone, fax machine, and whatever else you invest in should be able to help you grow your business or it's wasting your time and money.

Value is added by tools and activities that:

- Increase your sales.
- Lower your overhead.
- Enable you to get more done in less time.

Therefore, before you invest your time and money in new technology (or anything else), ask yourself the following three questions:

- Will this help make me more sales?
- Will it lower my overhead?
- Will it enable me to get more done in less time?

If the answer to all three questions is no, don't buy it or learn how to use it.

For example, like most men, I love gadgets. In my office, I have a computer, laser printer, telephone-answering machine, fax machine, modem, copy machine, personal organizer, and postage meter. There's no doubt in my mind that all of these tools provide payoffs to my business far in excess of the amount of time and money that I invest in them.

I also have a cellular phone that goes with me when I'm in my car or out of town. Given the nature of my business, there is no way I can justify it as a good business investment. It's convenient. It's great to have if my car breaks down or I get lost and need directions. But it doesn't bring in a dime and it's relatively expensive. I don't have to be on tap for my clients, friends, or business associates whenever they call.

Although I use the cellular phone to transact business from time to time, it's not the least-cost option. I usually stay in touch with my simple answering machine that has a beeperless remote, and check in periodically from the hotel or a pay phone when I'm on the road. From the dollars-and-cents standpoint, the pay phone and answering machine work just as well and are a whole lot cheaper.

For some, a cellular phone is an essential business tool. In my particular case, it's a convenience. It makes life easier and I can afford it, so I have it. There's nothing wrong with conveniences. Just don't confuse them with sound business investments. Remember that the smart tools of information technology are tools and nothing more. They're just a means to help you achieve your goals faster and more easily and cheaply. Don't buy anything unless you clearly understand how it will help you toward that end. To do otherwise is to fall prey to virtual stupidity.

SOME OTHER GENERAL THOUGHTS ABOUT SMART TOOLS

Any specific advice I might give you about choosing a particular kind of telephone, fax machine, or computer hardware or software would probably be obsolete by the time you read it. So I can only hope to give you some general guidelines for how to think about smart tools and what to look for as you choose the ones your business needs. Rest assured that when it comes to computers, whatever you buy today will seem Stone Age and woefully inadequate in a few short years. But there are some key points to keep in mind about smart tools.

First, they're essential if you hope to compete. In today's rapidly changing world, almost every business has to be customer-focused, flexible, and fast. In a solo business it's easy to be customer-focused and flexible. But speed in responding to customers and getting work out quickly usually requires smart tools. Customer requests for written information can be fulfilled in minutes with a fax machine. And a lucrative sales contract that once took days or weeks to sign and deliver can be executed in minutes via fax. You can't expect to win a race if your competition is in a new Mercedes SL and you're in a Model T Ford.

Second, use smart tools as an inexpensive alternative to hiring people or paying for services. My ten-year-old, hundred-dollar telephone-answering machine takes my calls 24 hours a day, 7 days a week, 365 days a year. It doesn't take coffee breaks or vacations, call in sick, ask for a raise, or call me while I'm on the road to tell me it's quitting. The total maintenance cost on the machine has been less then $10 to buy two cassette tapes in ten years.

Third, if you haven't already done so, *get a computer and get computer literate.* That's the most valuable piece of advice I can give you. A personal computer (PC) can be the best secretary, bookkeeper, and office manager you ever had. It can also be a great graphic designer, desktop publisher, financial planner, research assistant, you name it. I know that my computer does the work of at least one and perhaps two full-time employees in helping me run my business. And I know that there are numerous computer applications that I'm not using that could increase my productivity.

If you doubt the value of buying and learning how to use a PC, consider this. A 1994 national survey revealed that a professionally self-employed person with a PC had an average household income of almost $70,000. That was 42 percent more than an average self-employed person without a PC earned, and almost 65 percent more than the average U.S. household income. Are you willing to invest a few thousand dollars and a hundred hours of learning time to boost your income by that much? If your answer is no, you don't need information. You need ambition.

People who are computerphobic fear the wrong enemy. The real enemy is computer illiteracy and technophobia. User-friendliness is here, and there are tutors, classes, and videocassettes that can teach you what you need to know for a nominal fee. Anyone who is literate can become computer literate.

Fourth, most smart tools are becoming cheaper, easier to use, and more powerful with the passage of time. The laptop computer or personal digital assistant that you can't afford today will be much more affordable, powerful, easier to use, and perhaps an essential business tool a few short years from now. Make it a habit to stay informed and upgrade your investments in technology when they're worth it to you.

Finally, don't get railroaded into buying stuff you don't need or before you need it. From what we read in the media, it's easy to think that if you don't own the latest software, regularly surf the Internet, or have a page on the World Wide Web, the world is passing you by. Keep it in perspective. The reality is that most people still have trouble programming their VCRs. Just because it's the newest and latest doesn't make it a good investment. Let others spend their money, and learn from them. When you're convinced it's a good investment for you, go ahead.

THE ABCs OF CHOOSING YOUR FIRST PC

Purchasing your first personal computer and the proper software and learning to use them will probably be your most expensive and time-consuming venture into the world of smart tools. But as expensive, frustrating, and confusing as it may initially seem, it's definitely more than worth it.

When choosing your first PC, you need to find someone who knows enough about computers and the nature of your business to help you make intelligent buying decisions. Do you have a friend or know someone who is successful in a business similar to yours? Ask him how he likes his system and what he recommends.

Another possibility is to hire a computer consultant to help you pick out a system that's right for you and help you get it up and running. Once again, you need someone who understands your business needs and enough about available hardware and software to help you make good choices. With so many choices, it's easy to overspend on computers.

The right consultant can save you a lot of time, money, and frustration. Just be sure your consultant understands business needs and isn't a techie. Techies are intrigued by the state of the art and not the application. They're in love with technology, and most know little or nothing about business. The likely result is you'll end up buying a lot more hardware and software than you need and won't have a clue as to how to get the most value from them.

A third option is to have someone you know and trust recommend a local computer dealer to help you. The dealer should be one who will provide you with enough intelligent guidance and after-the-sale service to help get you off to a good start. A small retailer who wants your long-term business is your best bet if you go this route. While their prices will probably be higher, so will their level of service and support. Keep in mind that your goal isn't to get the most hardware and software for your dollar. You want the most productivity for your dollar, and higher-priced dealers with great service and support are often your best resource. Inasmuch as they, too, are a small business, odds are they will understand your computing needs.

Choosing the Right Hardware

When you're ready to purchase a PC, you have two major decisions and a bunch of smaller ones to make. The first and most important choice is whether to buy a computer with an IBM-compatible or Apple Macintosh operating system. Mac systems run Mac software. IBM-compatible systems run DOS and Windows software. IBM-compatible systems are less expensive and offer many more software and hardware choices. Mac systems are more expensive but are easier to learn. As time goes on, the difference in learning difficulty between the two systems is narrowing. It's also possible, but not always convenient, to run IBM-compatible programs and documents on Mac systems and vice versa. Hopefully, the day will soon come when all software will automatically run on all PCs.

The second major choice is whether to buy a desktop or portable computer. With a desktop, you get more computer power for your money and equipment that's easier to work with for long periods of time. With a portable, you get compactness and portability. Unless portability is very important and space is extremely scarce, your first computer should be a desktop.

These are other important choices you need to make when buying your first PC:

• The central processing unit (CPU), or microprocessor. This is the main brain of the computer. CPU chips are getting better and faster with every passing year. Buy the latest, fastest, and most powerful one you can afford, even though it may be obsolete in a few years.

• Hard-disc size. This is the computer's file cabinet, which stores all the programs and data that you'll create and use. In

1985 my first Macintosh had 512 kilobytes (512,000 bytes) of storage space, and it was state of the art. In 1989 my second Mac had 50 megabytes (50 million bytes) of storage. My current Mac has 250 megabytes, and some are recommending 500 megabytes and 1 gigabyte (1 billion bytes) for new machines. Check to see what's currently recommended before you buy.

• Floppy-disc drive. Any relatively new computer should come equipped with a 3.5-inch floppy-disc drive. Documents and programs stored outside of the computer are normally stored on floppy discs. Floppy discs are to computers what cassette tapes are to cassette players.

• RAM, or random access memory, size. This is where data and programs are stored in the computer as you work with them. The more RAM, the better the computer performs. Like hard discs, RAM storage is measured in megabytes, such as 4, 8, 16, or 32 megabytes. Check to see what's currently recommended before you buy.

• Expandability. Make sure you can increase the RAM storage and replace the CPU chip with a more powerful one if you need to. This will prevent you from having to buy a whole new computer to take advantage of the new software that will undoubtedly come along. You can increase hard-disc storage capacity with an additional external or internal disc drive.

• Monitor. Get at least a 14-inch monitor with a dot-pitch rating of 0.28 mm or less. The smaller the number, the sharper the picture. Don't skimp on the monitor. If you get a good one, it will last you for years, and you won't have to buy a new one when you buy your next computer.

• Modem. This is your on-ramp to the information highway. It connects your computer to on-line services. A modem with fax capabilities allows you to fax documents directly from your computer and receive faxes that can be printed or stored into memory. Some computers have built-in modems. The speed of the modem is measured in BPS, or bits per second, such as 14,400 BPS or 28,800 BPS. Find out what speeds are currently recommended before you buy.

• Sound. Make sure your computer comes with a good sound system or can be outfitted with one.

• CD-ROM drive. This allows your computer to play compact disc programs of sound, data, and visual images. If you get one, get a quad-speed drive. For most people, it's a good investment.

• Backup storage device. An absolute must for your system. It copies and stores whatever programs and data are stored on your hard disc. Someday, when you least expect it, your hard disc will crash, taking all that valuable information with it. Have a tape backup, external hard disc, or some other means to store your work.

• Keyboard and mouse. Plenty of different models are available, and they will probably come as standard equipment with your computer. If you have a choice, choose ones that feel natural and comfortable to you.

• Printer. You'll be creating documents to send to customers and prospects, so you want high-quality printing. Your choices are the less expensive but slower ink-jet printers and the faster but more expensive laser printers. For business-quality images, your printer should have a minimum resolution of 300 dots per inch. If high-quality graphics are or might someday be important, ask about the possibility of adding a postscript option to the printer.

Finally, stick with name brands and reputable dealers, and shop to get a good idea about current prices. It's a very competitive industry, and you have lots of choices. By limiting your choices to the major brands, you're almost guaranteed to get well-manufactured equipment.

Choosing the Software You Need

Software is simply the set of programs that enable you to use your computer to do what you want it to do. Therefore, before you spend a bundle on software, ask yourself, What's the most valuable thing I want this computer to do for me? Then make it your first priority to buy the best piece of software that enables you to do that and learn how to use it.

For example, I'm a writer, business consultant, and speaker. I create a lot of written documents in the form of manuscripts and correspondence. Over 80 percent of the work I do on my computer is word processing, and it's the primary reason that I bought my first computer. The most important thing my computer can do is help make me a better, more efficient writer and get correspondence out faster. So the first piece of software I bought and made it my business to learn how to use was Microsoft Word. That was over ten years ago and I'm currently using an updated version of it. To be sure, there's a lot more about Word that I don't know than I do know. But I know what I need to know to make money, and that's why I bought it. When I need to learn something new, I pull the Bible-size instruction manual off the shelf and learn it.

As with hardware, your choices of software will be good ones if you stick with reputable name brands. The particular types of basic software that you are likely to find most useful are as follows:

• Word processing. Brochures, manuscripts, posters, newsletters, you name it. If it involves the written word, a good word-processing program will make you look like a pro. I wrote four books by hand and gave the manuscripts to a typist before buying a computer and learning word processing. Now I wonder how I managed without it. In addition to checking your grammar and spelling, a good word-processing program is the ultimate rewrite tool. And rewriting is the secret to good writing. The two most popular programs are WordPerfect and Word.

• Financial management. Keep track of your daily revenues and expenses, write checks, calculate your taxes, make investments, and plan your financial future. Those are just a few things you can do with good financial-management software.

• Database. Keeping track of your customer and business contacts, managing your time, composing mailing lists, compiling an electronic phone-number file, and organizing information by categories are all examples of database applications.

• Communications. Used in conjunction with a modem, this type of software connects your computer via telephone with other computers and gives you access to every conceivable type of information. With popular on-line services, such as America Online, CompuServe, and Prodigy, you can research magazines and databases, surf the Internet, participate in discussion forums, and keep in touch with your friends and business colleagues through electronic mail (also known as E-mail). Each on-line service requires that you have its particular communications software.

Many new computers come equipped with a number of software programs. Just be sure that they will do what you need them to do before you go to the trouble of learning how to use them. And if you're considering buying a piece of new software, ask someone using it how easy it is to learn. It's also a good idea to buy software from a company or a dealer with a toll-free number you can call for advice and support if you need assistance.

One final piece of advice about computers: In the early days of learning to use the computer, you will undoubtedly make a bunch of mistakes, such as erasing files and documents that you wanted to keep. If it's a really important document, make a backup copy on an external floppy disc or print a copy of the document before closing the file. That way you won't have to worry about accidentally destroying the hours of hard thinking and work that you put into creating a letter, spreadsheet, financial document, report, chapter of a book, or whatever.

OTHER SMART TOOLS WITH HIGH POTENTIAL PAYOFFS

I'm a great believer in getting a computer and putting it to work in your business. But I don't believe that it's your most essential smart tool. The most essential tool with the greatest payoff is the oldest and cheapest of all:

Your telephone.

While you may consider it elaborating on the obvious, you need to give some conscious thought and planning to choosing an effective telephone system. More specifically, you need to determine how many lines you'll need, what type of business telephone to buy, and how to handle incoming calls when you aren't there to take them.

Once again, you can get carried away with a multitude of bells and whistles and buy far more gadgetry than you need. Unless you live alone, I strongly recommend having at least one separate business line. I have two. The first line is used for telephone calls, and it's my published number. The second is primarily for faxing and on-line computer usage. I also use the fax line for placing outgoing calls, which keeps the first line open for incoming calls.

If you have two lines, you'll want a two-line telephone. If you need portability, consider buying a two-line cordless telephone. I use a corded two-line telephone with speaker-phone capability in my office. The speaker phone is handy when you call a business and get put on hold for long periods of time. It frees you to work on other tasks while waiting. And be sure to check the telephone for voice quality and reception volume before you buy it. All telephones are not created equal.

When it comes to taking your incoming calls when you aren't available, you have several basic options. One is a telephone answering machine. Another is to hire an answering service. A third is to use the local telephone company's message service, which gives you the basic features of an answering machine for a small monthly fee. Whatever method you choose, keep this thought in mind: *Whoever or whatever answers your business line is probably the first contact that customers and potential customers will have with your business.* It's essential that your message or the person taking your calls project and reinforce the image you want customers to have about your business. If you use an answering machine, buy one whose outgoing message has excellent playback quality. Make a friendly but professional-sounding outgoing message. If you use an answering service, call yourself up periodically to ensure that your calls are being handled properly. Your telephone is the lifeline of your business. Treat it as such.

Get the Fax

In early 1988 someone called me requesting information and asked, "Do you have a fax machine?" I replied, "No, I don't," and thought to myself, Why in the hell would I want a fax machine? Was I ever wrong! It didn't take me long to see the error of my ways and I quickly went out and bought one. The investment has repaid me many times over. Since that time the cost of fax machines has plummeted, and today they're standard office equipment.

Assuming your business has need for a fax, you have two basic choices to make. The first is to decide if you need a PC with a fax modem, a separate fax machine, or both. I personally find fax modems alone inadequate for my needs and have a separate fax. With a fax modem, you can fax only documents stored in the memory of your computer. Another advantage of a separate fax is that it can double as a copier.

If you decide to buy a separate fax, you have to choose between plain-paper and thermal-paper models. I've had one of each. The thermal-paper models are cheaper in price and maintenance, but you have to deal with thermal paper. The plain-paper varieties are more expensive, and periodically you have to buy a toner cartridge for them. The thing that drove me to buy a plain-paper fax wasn't the thermal paper. The particular machine I had didn't have a paper cutter. Whenever someone sent me a fax of several pages, I had a long stream of paper all over my office floor and a hassle to deal with. If you buy a thermal fax, be sure it has a paper cutter.

Like telephones and telephone-answering devices, fax machines come in a multitude of price ranges and with various features. Some have higher halftone definition for sending photographs and graphic designs. Some have a memory that will capture documents if the machine runs out of paper while you're away. Some can be programmed to send documents overnight when long-distance rates are cheapest. Some have a broadcasting feature that allows you to send the same fax to numerous places. For most home offices, a basic thermal fax is all you need. If your business grows to the point that you need all those extra features, you'll be able to afford a new one.

Multiuse Smart Tools

With the market for home-based business equipment booming, it's not surprising to see a number of new products that combine the features of several smart tools in one. My first fax machine was also a telephone and digital answering machine with beeperless remote. One of the best breakthroughs in home office products has been the combination of fax machine, copy machine, computer printer, and sometimes a scanner into one appliance that is sold for a fraction of the cost of separate pieces of equipment. In addition to the obvious cost saving, the combination product requires far less space, which is a big benefit for most home offices.

But like most several-in-one appliances, there are disadvantages, too. The first is that these machines are usually a compromise, and you don't get everything you'd get by buying separate products. For example, the printer may not be as fast or offer a resolution that is as sharp as an expensive, stand-alone printer.

Another disadvantage to consider is that when the combination product breaks, your office shuts down because you lose copying, printing, and faxing capabilities. One way around this problem is to buy from a dealer who will provide you with a loaner while your machine is being repaired. For many, if not most, home-based businesses, combination copier/fax/printers are an excellent buy and worthy of serious consideration. Look at several makes and models before buying to be sure you get the features that are important to you.

Another combination device that will become more important in the future is the personal digital assistant, or PDA. This device combines wireless communications and computing devices in a pocket-size package. The objective is to create an all-in-one, portable smart tool. With the ultimate PDA, the user would be able to:

- Place and receive telephone calls;
- Send and receive faxes and E-mail;

- Access on-line services;
- Do word processing and other computer tasks;
- Scan documents into memory;
- Make handwritten notes;
- And, in short, communicate with anyone and anything from anywhere.

Early models have failed to live up to the hype and were the butt of a lot of stand-up-comic routines. But if the past is prologue, the technology will get better, the problems will be solved, and the PDAs will eventually become an essential smart tool for people on the go. Remember, it wasn't so long ago that people were saying, "To err is human. To really mess things up, you need a computer." Funny, you don't hear that anymore.

A Final Thought

In addition to the tools I've mentioned, there are others that you can use to multiply yourself and save time. A beeper is an inexpensive way to know when others are trying to reach you. Pocket-size electronic organizers are a great multifunction tool for storing names and addresses, keeping track of expenses, making notes to yourself, and performing calculations. A copier will save the time traveling to and from the copy center. And a postage meter will prevent you from overpaying on postage and waiting in line at the post office.

While you might like to start your business with all those tools, chances are you won't be able to afford them all at once. Start with those that will help you make the best use of your time. But whatever you do, start investing in smart tools. They're a fast, inexpensive way to increase your productivity.

10

Money: How Millionaires Get to Be Millionaires

> I'm opposed to millionaires, but it would be dangerous to offer me the position.
>
> —MARK TWAIN

In a 1991 survey, *Woman's Day* magazine asked women if they would rather be rich, beautiful, famous, or younger. An overwhelming 71 percent said they'd take the money and run. And people are forever saying, "Money isn't important."

The fact is that money *is* important. No, money isn't the most important thing in life. It isn't a substitute for good health, self-esteem, good times, peace of mind, love, or friendship. It can't buy the self-satisfaction that comes from doing a good deed or outstanding work. And while money is often used as a measure of success, it should never be confused with success. People (such as drug dealers, con artists, thieves, and mobsters) who get rich by harming others are miserable failures as human beings.

But while money may not buy happiness, it sure can chase the hell out of misery. Money is a great problem solver. It's not what it does for you. It's what it delivers you from. The best thing about having money is not having to worry about it. Study after study confirms that people with money are happier. With financial independence comes more freedom, more power to do good, more choice, less stress, and an overall better life. As Woody Allen put it, "Money is better than poverty, if only for financial reasons."

LIFESTYLES OF THE RICH AND NOT SO FAMOUS

In 1994 there were 2.3 million U.S. households with a net worth of at least $1 million. Research on people who accumulate such a net worth yields some interesting surprises. First, they aren't who you think they are. Most millionaires don't wear a gold Rolex and designer clothes or drive expensive foreign cars. They're more likely to wear a Timex and everyday clothing and drive a pickup truck or an American sedan. They appear to be Mr. and Mrs. Average American.

Second, most don't live in super-expensive homes. Many live in the same modest homes they occupied when their net worth was far less. They see no point in spending the bulk of their fortune on a fancy house when a less expensive one serves them just as well and costs less to maintain. They tend to have simple rather than extravagant tastes, and they enjoy a lifestyle of moderation and stability.

Most millionaires are men in their fifties or sixties who have married only once and are still married to the same woman. While some doctors and lawyers become millionaires, the more typical millionaire is a small-business owner who got rich working six days a week for 30 years. At age 60, there are twice as many millionaire salesmen as millionaire doctors. And less than one percent of all millionaires are athletes and entertainers.

In short, most millionaires are not into conspicuous consumption. That's one key reason they become millionaires. The other key reason is that they are heavily involved in three other activities: working, saving, and investing.

THE SECRET IS IN THE SIMPLICITY

Whenever I tell people that it's possible for them to become a millionaire working from home, I usually get an answer like, "Yeah, right. Which lottery am I going to win?" But I'm personally convinced that it's not only possible but highly probable that most future millionaires will be micropreneurs working from home. Here's why.

The financial advantage of owning a one-person, home-based business can be enormous. You have no one to pay but yourself. You have no additional rent or utilities. While a large corporation is delighted to have 20 percent of its revenue going to profit, a huge percentage of the home-based business's revenue goes straight to the bottom line. That's the magic of the one-person, home-based business—simplicity.

To illustrate, let's consider two hypothetical businesses. Business number one is a typical small business with a very healthy 25 percent profit margin and Business number two is a home-based, one-person business with a profit margin of 80 percent. To earn a dollar for its owner, Business number one must sell $4.00 worth of goods and services while Business number two must sell only $1.25.

The typical small business is saddled with a huge amount of fixed overhead, such as rent, utilities, salaries, and inventory. Consequently, it must generate a continuous, healthy amount of sales just to break even and keep the doors open. On the other hand, a one-person home-based information business has practically no fixed costs. If the sales go flat for a month, you don't get stressed. You get a vacation! You don't have to worry about laying people off or borrowing money to pay your business bills. You're free to concentrate on creating new ways to bring in more business. And because you aren't stressed, you come up with better ideas.

Of course, if you want to make tens of millions of dollars, you aren't likely to do it in a one-person business. But the road to financial independence and your first million or so may come much more quickly and with a lot less stress if you go solo.

IT'S NOT WHAT YOU MAKE THAT COUNTS

When it comes to money, the mind-set you need to become a millionaire is this: *It's not what you make that counts. It's what you keep.*

Your ultimate goal is not to maximize your gross income or net income. Your goal is to accumulate a net worth of at least $1 million. Net worth is simply the difference between what you own and what you owe. It's the dollar value of your wealth. For example, if you own $100,000 worth of assets and you owe $20,000 in outstanding debts, your net worth is $80,000. When the sum total of what you own is worth a million dollars more than your debts, congratulations! You're a millionaire.

Calculating your net worth is very simple. First, add up the current dollar value of everything you own. Such items include:

- Cash in checking and savings accounts, credit unions, or money-market funds.
- The cash value of your life insurance.
- Your home and any other real estate holdings.
- Any stocks, bonds, mutual funds, certificates of deposit, government securities, or other investments.
- Pension or retirement plans.
- Cars, boats, motorcycles, or other vehicles.
- Personal items, such as clothing, jewelry, home furnishings, and appliances.
- Collectibles, such as art or antiques.
- Your business if you were to sell it.
- Anything else of value that you own.

Once you have the total current value of what you own, add up the total amount of all debts that you currently owe. These include the total amount due on:

- The mortgage on your house or any real estate holdings.
- Credit cards.
- Car loans.
- Personal loans.
- Educational loans.
- Life insurance loans.
- Home equity loans.
- Accounts payable in your business.
- Any other debts.

Subtract what you owe from what you own, and that's your net worth. If you're a long way from a million, don't feel depressed or alone. The median net worth of U.S. households (half have more, half have less) is about $38,000.

Millionaires become millionaires by focusing on building their net worth. If you make a million and spend it all, you aren't building net worth. You're just living like a king for the time being. Wealth isn't created from what you make. It's created from what you keep. To make a million as a micropreneur, you need two basic things:

1. High income. You need to create a business that's capable of producing an after-tax income well above your living expenses.
2. A commitment to saving and investment. You need to keep your living expenses low, save the excess income, and invest it where it can work to multiply your net worth as you continue to work in the business.

Let's look at some income and money-management strategies that have worked for me and will get you on the fast track to your first million.

INCOME-MAXIMIZING STRATEGIES

It's important to be passionate about your business and enjoy it. But let's be realistic. If you're going to make a million, the business needs to be a lean, mean, money machine. The following six strategies are the ones I've found to be the most valuable for maximizing income.

1. Invest in Knowledge and Technology.

It's a cliché but true that the best investment is in yourself. No matter what business you choose, become an ardent student and engross yourself in learning all you can about what it takes to become a leader in your business. In today's fast-paced business world, it's more essential than ever and will repay you many times over.

The second-best business investment for a micropreneur is in the smart tools of the information age. Technology enables you to multiply yourself without the additional time and expense of hiring and managing other people. You can devote all of your work time to productive tasks.

If you have ever owned or managed a business, I don't have to remind you that employees can consume an enormous amount of time, energy, and money. As my CPA once told me, "Michael, you've created the perfect business. You have no payroll, no employee headaches, no debts, no inventory, no rent, and you're making a lot of money."

2. Control Costs Relentlessly.

Call me Scrooge if you like, but here's an axiom that will help you make your first million a lot faster: *Don't spend a dime on anything unless you absolutely have to.*

Every dollar you don't spend on overhead goes straight to the bottom line. And every dollar you save and invest goes to increasing your net worth. The problem is that we tend to spend more money when times are good. It's probably a throwback to the paycheck mentality. We believe that if we make a lot this year, we'll make even more next year. Failure to jealously monitor and control the costs of doing business has led many an entrepreneur down the path to financial ruin.

I've seen it happen numerous times in the business of professional speaking. Vince Verbal has the gift of gab. Audiences are captivated by his message. Corporations and professional associations pay him handsomely to hear his story. He has a great year and thinks he's on his way to the big time. He moves from Middleburg, USA, to La Jolla, Newport Beach, or Honolulu and buys an expensive home. He hires a staff and rents a large office. He spends a small fortune on office equipment and marketing materials to promote himself. But a funny thing happens on the way to the big time.

It seems that Vince's audiences have heard his message once and aren't eager to hear it again. Unless he keeps finding new audiences, all that newly created overhead is going to wipe him out. Consequently, he ends up spending even more money on marketing. Desperate to pay his bills, he travels all over the country to speak to anyone who will pay him for any fee he can get. It's not uncommon to find the Vince Verbals of the world broke, burned out, in poor health, and aged far beyond their years in a few short years. If Vince had stayed in Middleburg and kept his overhead low, he could be financially independent today.

When is the best time to control costs? Today and every day. Never let up. It's the little things that add up to big-time overhead—an extra telephone line here, a part-time worker there. Whenever you're deciding on purchasing a piece of equipment, estimate both the optimistic and pessimistic amount of money you think it will save you. Then ask yourself the questions proposed by the American Society of Value Engineers:

- What is it?
- What does it do?
- What does it cost?
- What else does the job?
- What does that cost?

Any good football coach will tell you that offense sells tickets and defense wins championships. Similarly, as a micropreneur, sales bring in business, and cost control wins your financial freedom. Stay lean.

3. Let the PIGs Set You Free.

The PIGs I'm talking about have nothing to do with pork. It's an acronym for passive income generators. Those are products and services that go on selling with little or no extra work on your part. For example, every time you pay your telephone bill or send in a check to renew your auto insurance, you're generating income for the telephone and insurance companies that requires little effort on their part. That's a PIG for them. When you pay your monthly rent to the landlord, that's a PIG for him. When an oil company digs a well that goes on gushing oil for years, that's a PIG for it.

In the business of writing, consulting, and speaking, PIGs make a big difference in my income. In speaking and consulting, there is no passive income. If I don't work, I don't get paid. But as an author of books, audiotapes, and videotapes, I get plenty of passive income. I still receive, with no additional effort on my part, royalties from books I wrote over 15 years ago. And I still receive income from audio- and videotapes that were recorded years ago. The more PIGs I create, the more money I make with little or no additional effort on my part. This frees me to use my time to speak, consult, create new PIGS, or do anything else I want.

Look at your business and ask yourself, What products or services can I create that will continue to generate income with little or no additional effort on my part? A time-management consultant I know created a special wall calendar that his clients purchase every year. It's a big PIG for him. A landscape architect sells maintenance contracts to his customers for a yearly fee. He then subcontracts the work to gardeners who do the actual work, and he keeps a percentage. When customers renew their contracts, that's a PIG for the architect. If you don't have any PIGs, create some. One day the PIGs will set you free.

4. Charge What the Market Will Bear.

When potential clients call and ask, "How much do you charge to speak?" I usually tell them, "The speech is free. I charge for airline abuse." Of course, I'm joking, although I do charge less to speak in my hometown.

There are no hard-and-fast rules for pricing what you sell. It's largely a matter of trial and error until you find a level that works for you. How much time you want to put in, what you want to be paid for your time, and what your fixed and variable costs of doing business will be are all necessary considerations. But the most important consideration is simply what people are willing to pay. And what people are willing to pay is based on the perccived value of what you sell.

Pricing products is usually easier than pricing services because there is less latitude. If there are a number of similar products, chances are that your products will do best selling in the range of the normal going rate. But pricing individual services allows a lot more latitude because customers' perceptions about what they are willing to pay can vary greatly. Years ago when I was a fledgling writer and speaker, I was thrilled the first time I was paid $1,000 for a speech. A few months later someone called to inquire about my speaking services. When I quoted a fee of $1,000, he replied, "You must not be very good."

There's a very important lesson here. Don't sell yourself short. You may be worth a whole lot more to your clients than you think. Once you know you can do a high-quality job and are willing to guarantee your work, don't be afraid to ask a healthy price. While you'll be too expensive for some, others will think you're worth it and then some. People value what they pay for.

For example, several years ago someone called and wanted to know what I would charge to do a seminar for a company on the other side of the world. Because of the large amount of time and travel, I quoted double my normal price only to be told, "That's awfully low." But whatever you decide to charge, your fee structure should have integrity. One way to give yourself a black eye in the market is to charge one client one price and another client a totally different price. People talk.

In deciding what your prices should be, talk to other people in your line of work, and based on your qualifications and experience, pick a price for your services. Initially, it's better to err on the low side. Then let supply and demand take over. If you have too much work, raise your prices. Some people double their prices and find they make more money because the increase in revenue more than offsets the amount lost through customer defections. If you're delivering perceived value, you're going to make money. Your job is to get top dollar for the value you provide.

5. Be Thorough about Collections.

As one sage put it, "Making deals is so much trash if, my friend, you don't get no cash." Whatever you do, don't get a reputation for being soft on customers who don't pay their bills.

Perhaps I've been fortunate, but it has been my experience that clients who won't pay their bills without prodding are a rarity. I can count the number of seriously delinquent clients I've had on one hand and have several fingers left over. And I've had to take legal action only once. The overwhelming majority of people are honest, ethical, and pay their bills on time, and the deadbeats are a small minority. But there are a number of things you can do to prevent overdue accounts. One is to demand payment in full in advance. One speaker I know quotes his fee 10 percent above what he wants and offers his clients a 10 percent discount if they pay in advance. As a result, he has no accounts receivable. If you don't feel comfortable asking for payment up front, ask for a 50 percent deposit. Another option is to have a credit-card merchant account and ask for payment by credit card.

On a major sale, always get the terms and conditions in writing, including the total cost and schedule of when payment is due. This will prevent a lot of misunderstandings and make collecting far easier if you have to resort to legal recourse. If you deliver the goods, send your bill, and fail to get paid, don't procrastinate. The longer you delay, the smaller the odds of ever being paid. Call the client and find out if there is a problem. Is he satisfied with your work? If there are some extenuating circumstances that delay payment, work out a schedule that is mutually agreeable.

Unfortunately, no matter how firm or fair you try to be, sooner or later you'll have a client who simply ignores your requests for payment. If that's the case, hire a collection agency or attorney in the state where the client resides and pay them a percentage for collecting. Consider it a necessary cost of doing business.

6. Hire the Best Tax and Financial Adviser You Can.

Unless your field is accounting and finance, don't make the mistake of trying to be your own financial adviser and tax accountant. The laws and intricacies of the tax and financial world are sciences unto themselves. The untold hours you devote to trying to be your own accountant are hours you can't devote to doing the actual work that brings in the money.

Please don't misunderstand me. I'm not saying that you can be financially ignorant and succeed. It's possible, but I don't recommend it. A good working knowledge of accounting principles is valuable and will help you to work better with a CPA. The more you understand, the better. But it's been my experience that the money you pay a good CPA to help you with tax- and business-planning matters is an excellent investment. CPAs help you uncover deductions you may not be aware of. They can work with you to formulate a strategy for legally paying the minimum amount of tax. They can advise you on how to set up pension plans that will lower your taxable income and allow your retirement money to grow tax-deferred.

Millionaires become millionaires because they understand the difference between frugality and being penny-wise and pound-foolish. Don't try to be your own financial adviser unless it's your area of expertise. Good financial advisers will save/earn you far more than the fees they charge.

One final word of caution: By financial advisers, I mean people (such as certified public accountants) who are paid for the services they perform and not the products they sell. The financial world is full of "experts" who, in fact, aren't very knowledgeable. Their primary purpose is not to help you but to sell you their products and make a fat commission.

MONEY-MANAGEMENT STRATEGIES

The actor George Raft once explained how he blew about $10 million: "Part of the loot went for gambling, part for horses, and part for women. The rest I spent foolishly." There are two factors to getting rich—making money and managing it. The latter is far more important. If you wait until you're rich to manage your money, odds are you'll never be rich. But given enough time and the application of a few simple money-management strategies, virtually anyone can become a millionaire.

Having a business that's generating a healthy income, while important, is only half the battle. Whether or not you become financially independent hinges on your commitment to saving and investing. Here are four strategies that have helped me and will help you toward that end.

1. Pay Yourself First.

It's advice that's as old as the ages. You've heard it before and you'll no doubt hear it again. Pay yourself first. Take a minimum of 10 percent of your income off the top and save it. As Ben Franklin said over two hundred years ago, "If you would be wealthy, think of saving as well as getting."

I can hear you saying, "But I can't save ten percent of my income." Here's my answer: Can't means won't. The truth is, you're used to living on a certain income, and to save 10 percent means sacrificing something. Look at the nice chunk of money you give the government every year. You do it for one simple reason: You have no choice. You pay your taxes or risk being fined and/or imprisoned.

And speaking of the government, don't make the mistake of thinking your retirement is secure because of Social Security, Medicare, and other government programs. The fact is that there may be no Social Security or Medicare by the time you reach retirement age. At best, it will be a meager subsistence. And how would you like to be old, broke, in poor health, and at the mercy of the government during your senior years? Fail to save and, unless you die prematurely, it's your guaranteed fate. Save and invest for your own retirement. Don't count on the government, and if you get government benefits you'll be that much better off.

Some people, such as the Japanese, think nothing of saving 15 or 20 percent of their income and do it as a matter of habit. All citizens of Singapore are required by law to save 25 percent of their salary, and their employer is forced to match it. If a Singaporean buys a house or condominium, his monthly payment is deducted from his forced savings so his take-home pay is unchanged. At age 55, the Singaporean citizen receives a lump-sum payment equal to 50 percent of every dollar he has earned, less deductions for house payments, plus compound interest. As a result, the citizens of Singapore are in great financial shape at 55 with decades of life ahead of them. We Americans live in the richest country in the history of the world, yet our savings rate typically hovers around 5 percent. Can't means won't. So have a plan to save a certain percentage of your annual income with a target date of attaining a net worth of $1 million. And stick to your plan.

2. Put the Power of Compound Interest to Work.

It may surprise you to learn that Albert Einstein didn't think nuclear power was his most notable discovery. Word has it that he believed his most notable discovery was the wealth-building power of compound interest. How I wish someone had sat me down as a young person and told me about the power of compound interest and the Rule of 72! Once again, it's something I didn't learn until I was well into my forties.

Becoming a millionaire looks much easier when you know the Rule of 72. This simple rule states that when you invest your money, 72 divided by the annual rate of return of the investment equals the approximate number of years it takes to double your money. For example, an investment that pays:

- 3 percent per year takes 24 years to double your money ($72 \div 3 = 24$).
- 6 percent per year takes 12 years to double your money ($72 \div 6 = 12$).
- 8 percent per year takes 9 years to double your money ($72 \div 8 = 9$).
- 9 percent per year takes 8 years to double your money ($72 \div 9 = 8$).
- 12 percent per year takes 6 years to double your money ($72 \div 12 = 6$).
- 18 percent per year takes 4 years to double your money ($72 \div 18 = 4$).

Obviously, the higher the rate of return, the more money your investment earns for you. But most people don't realize the enormous impact that a difference of a few percentage points can make over a long period of time. For example, let's look at $2,000 invested at rates of 6, 15, and 20 percent.

RATE OF RETURN	VALUE AFTER 12 YEARS	VALUE AFTER 24 YEARS
6%	$4,024	$8,098
15%	$10,701	$52,750
20%	$17,832	$158,994

You may have thought I was exaggerating when I said that almost anyone can become a millionaire. Well, here's an example using the power of compound interest that proves my point. If a person at age 18 started saving $3.00 a day and invested it in a mutual fund that averaged a 10 percent annual return (an easily attainable rate), at age 65 he or she would be worth $1,153,727. Saving $3.00 a day would have a negligible impact on the person's current lifestyle and an enormous impact on his or her retirement lifestyle.

Here's another example that illustrates the value of investing early in life. Jack and Jill are both 24 years old. Jack invests nothing until age 30 and then begins investing $2,000 per year for 35 years for a total investment of $70,000. Jill invests $2,000 per year starting at age 24 for six years for a total investment of only $12,000. After age 30 she invests nothing. Assuming both their investments earn an average annual return of 10 percent, both Jack and Jill will be worth $596,254 at age 65. By starting six years earlier, Jill gets the same payoff as Jack at age 65 with only 17 percent of the investment. If you have children, please, please, please teach them about the power of compound interest.

Obviously, if you start later in life, you have to invest more and get a higher rate of return to accumulate a million. But it's still well within the realm of possibility. For example, if you invest $10,000 per year at an average annual return of 10 percent, it takes 25 years to make a million. But no matter when you start, keep the Rule of 72 in mind and put the power of compound interest to work for you. It's your biggest potential PIG of all. A penny saved may be a penny earned. But a penny well invested will someday be worth a lot of dollars.

3. If It Floats, Flies, or Flirts, Lease It.

One evening I was watching David Letterman, and his guest was Terry Bradshaw. Always entertaining, Terry told of a friend of his who started making money. And what did he do with his money? First he bought a boat. Then he bought a plane. And he went through a couple of bad marriages, too. After having done all this, he told Terry that he had learned a very important lesson in life: "If it floats, flies, or flirts, lease it."

Expensive toys are just that—expensive. And as the old saying goes, "Love is grand. Divorce is twenty grand." (Or a lot more, depending on how much you're worth.) Once you start making good money, save and invest it. Don't be a miser, but don't feel compelled to splurge just because you have it. Go on living for a few years at the level you've become accustomed to and salt away the rest. Pay off your mortgage and the rest of your debts. Tax-shelter and tax-defer everything you can.

If you want to get married, great. Protect your assets with a prenuptial agreement. Most of our divorce laws are woefully antiquated and were written for a different era, when most women were homemakers and divorce rates were far lower. If your partner loves you for you, he or she will gladly sign a prenuptial agreement. You don't want someone marrying you for your money, and you definitely don't want him or her divorcing you for it. A prenuptial agreement prevents both.

You may be thinking that all this advice doesn't sound very romantic, exciting, or fun. But keep this in mind. With a million in your back pocket, you're free to spend your days doing any legal thing you want to do. Think about that the next time your alarm goes off on Monday morning.

4. You Only Have to Get Rich Once.

When I was in my twenties I heard an older man say, "It doesn't take a smart man to make money, but it takes a smart one to keep it." At the time I thought it was a dumb remark. Today I'm convinced it's true. Wise people learn how to protect, preserve, and grow their fortunes with the ultimate goal of complete financial freedom. Fools squander theirs.

The reality is that you only have to get rich once if you work it right. You need to decide what you want your money to do for you and how to enjoy it without frittering it away. In short, you need good financial advice. So hire a financial planner to work with and advise you on where to invest your money for maximum return. A good financial planner can be one of your most valuable business partners.

11

Partners Make the Difference

> I make progress by having people around me who are
> smarter than I am—and listening to them. And I as-
> sume that everyone is smarter about something than
> I am.
>
> —HENRY KAISER

An old Moslem fable tells the story of a blind man and a crippled man, both of whom had been lost in a forest for as long
as they could remember. One day they stumbled onto each
other, and the blind man said, "I cannot see my way out." The
crippled man replied, "I cannot get up to walk out." Then
suddenly the crippled man said, "I've got it! If you lift me up
on your shoulders, I'll tell you where to walk." And together
they found their way out of the forest. It's an excellent example of partnering.

While the independence and freedom of working in a
home-based solo business is wonderful, always keep this
point in mind: Success in any business is based on effective
interdependence.

We need customers to have a business. We need vendors to
supply us with raw materials, information, or inventory. We
need mentors, professional colleagues, experts in our field,
and confidants to share ideas with and learn from. We need

agents and retailers to market our products effectively. We need legal advisers to protect our interests and keep us within the bounds of the law. We need insurance advisers to provide financial protection from the unwanted and unexpected. We need financial advisers for tax-planning purposes, to keep our business on a sound financial footing, and for personal financial planning. And last but not least, we need the support of family and friends as we go about the task of building a thriving business. Nobody does it alone. Once again, let me make this point: The day you start believing that *you* are the business is the beginning of the end of your business.

It's a cliché when corporate chieftains state, "Our people are our most important asset." In a solo business, your partners are your most important asset. And they will make or break you, depending on their own personal abilities, their integrity, and how effectively they work with you. How to find the right partners and work with them is what a solo business is all about.

GUIDELINES FOR EFFECTIVE PARTNERING

If you were to ask a hundred people what kind of partners they wanted to work with, practically everyone would list the same attributes. We all like to work with people who are:

- honest and trustworthy;
- excellent at what they do;
- more valuable to us than the money they charge;
- reliable and dependable about delivering what they promise;
- accessible and supportive when we need their help; and
- reasonable and enjoyable to work with.

You can increase the odds of finding those kinds of partners by doing the following two things:

1. *Be the kind of partner you would like to work with,* and
2. *Treat your partners like the people you want them to become.*

By being a consistently honest, cooperative, trustworthy person, you establish a reputation as someone others want to work with, and you'll have no shortage of partners to choose from. And the more choices you have, the better the odds of choosing excellent ones.

The reason for treating people like the people we want them to become is that people, for better or worse, tend to live up to our expectations. If you have ever taught a class, coached a team, managed a business, or been in any leadership role, you probably already know this. Through our words, deeds, and actions, we tell people how we expect them to behave, and they tend to do just that. The more you treat your partners as honest, competent, and trustworthy, the harder they will work to prove you're right. Unfortunately, the opposite is equally true.

But please don't misunderstand me. Simply being a great partner and expecting the best from others are no guarantees that you'll have only great partners. The plain fact is that some people are incompetent. Others are unreliable. Still others are dishonest, and nothing you do can ever change that. Don't be naive. As an old Russian proverb states, "Trust but verify." Check references, ask others, and verify that any potential partners are, in fact, reliable, trustworthy, and honest. Success in any kind of partnership is part being a good partner and part finding a good partner.

Given that you have high expectations for yourself and others, here are some additional general guidelines for finding and working effectively with partners:

First, think win/win and look for partners who are win/win-oriented. No relationship will work unless there's something in it for both parties. Like the blind man and the crippled man in the fable, the best partnerships are symbiotic. By working together, both partners benefit in ways they would not have by working alone.

Second, in all partnerships, including those with customers, strive wherever possible for a long-term ongoing relationship. In the long run, it will be cheaper and more beneficial for both you and them.

Third, before you consider entering into a working relationship with any partner, check his reputation in the marketplace. Aligning yourself with partners who have shady reputations is one sure way to hurt your own image. Choose partners who are known for integrity and delivering value.

Finally, while you don't have to like all the people you work with, you should be able to respect, trust, and communicate with them. If a lawyer or financial adviser insists on speaking to you in legalese or financialese, and you can't understand him, he isn't the partner for you.

CHOOSING YOUR PROFESSIONAL ADVISORY TEAM

Perhaps a better name for a professional advisory team is "peace-of-mind team." The basic job of the members of that team is to keep you out of legal and financial trouble while you concentrate on growing your business. So you must select these partners with great care. If they give you bad advice that gets you in trouble, you're going to be the one held accountable.

There are four professional advisers you need to consider having on your team: an accountant, an insurance agent, a lawyer, and a financial planner. You don't have to be self-employed to have a professional advisory team, and you may already have one. If you're satisfied with your advisers' services, that's great. Just keep in mind that as you make the transition from employee to micropreneur, their role will become increasingly important in determining your long-term success.

One of the best ways to start your search for good professional advisers is to ask other successful home-based business owners to recommend an accountant or insurance agent they have been working with. Also, a number of accountants, lawyers, and financial planners are themselves micropreneurs who have firsthand knowledge of your type of legal and financial needs You might want to attend a meeting of one of your local home-based-business associations and ask for referrals.

Get several names of each type of adviser you're looking for and interview them. Don't be intimidated by credentials. Remember, you're the customer. What can they do for you? What kind of rapport do you have with them? What other clients do they represent? What are their specialties and strengths? What are their weaknesses? What do they charge? How will they be more valuable to you than the money they charge?

Expect to pay a healthy price for good information, representation, advice, or quality products. Just because you pay a low price doesn't mean you're getting great value. The best people always charge top dollar but are almost always worth more than they are paid. That having been said, don't pay for anything you don't need or understand. You probably don't need a lawyer or CPA on retainer if you're just starting out. Pay them by the job.

If You Don't Have a CPA, Get One

I'm a great believer in hiring the best financial advice you can find. A certified public accountant isn't your least-cost route to financial and tax planning advice. You can hire a public accountant or tax preparer or do it all yourself. But choosing a CPA greatly lessens the odds of your employing an incompetent or a charlatan to advise you in the all-important financial matters of running your business. A good CPA will:

• Help you decide which legal form of business (sole proprietorship, corporation, etc.) is best for you.

• Work with you to prepare your tax returns and ensure that you pay the legal minimum amount of tax.

• Assess the financial strengths and weaknesses of your business. You need to know what's making you money and what's costing you money. A good CPA can tell you.

• Recommend a retirement program, such as a Simplified Employee Pension (SEP), a Keogh Plan, or an Individual Retirement Account (IRA), that will enable your retirement savings to grow tax-deferred.

• Greatly lessen the odds of your tax return being audited and represent you to the IRS if your return is audited.

• Recommend types of insurance coverage that you need and how much.

To become a CPA, a person must hold a college degree and pass a series of very rigorous exams. Our current tax system is a ridiculous maze of complex rules that are forever changing. A good CPA will save you more than he charges, not to mention the anguish of tax preparation.

You Can't Afford to Be Uninsured

Drop the ball on insurance coverage just once, and the game could well be over. Becoming a micropreneur means you need more than just life, health, homeowner's, and auto insurance, all of which you may already have. You need personal and product liability insurance in case someone sues you. You need disability insurance until you become financially independent. You need business insurance because your homeowner's policy may not cover damage to your business.

I recommend buying all of your insurance from one agent. By doing that, you become a more important customer, and it's in that agent's best interest to see to it that you're well covered and well served. As for choosing an agent, there are basically two kinds. Independent agents represent a number of companies and can shop for the best prices and coverage to fit your needs. Exclusive agents sell the insurance of only one company. While their prices aren't always the cheapest, if you choose an agent who represents a large, reputable company, you aren't faced with the problem of the company going belly-up and your being left uninsured. With so many insurance frauds, scams, and failures, you can't afford to buy insurance from any company with less than a superior rating.

If you're looking for a good agent, ask your CPA whom he would recommend. A good agent won't sell you coverage that you don't need and will check with you regularly to see that your coverage is up-to-date and sufficient.

Get a Lawyer Before You Need One

There's no shortage of lawyers. In fact, word has it that medical schools are considering using lawyers instead of white rats for laboratory experiments because:

- they're more plentiful;
- you don't get attached to them;
- they're willing to do things that rats won't do.

There's also no shortage of lawyer jokes, but when you're in dire need of a lawyer, it's no laughing matter. If that happens, and you don't know where to turn for legal help, your options are limited. You can pick a name out of the Yellow Pages, call one of the personal-injury sharks who advertise on TV, or ask a friend whose brother-in-law is a lawyer.

The best time to find a reputable attorney is before you need one. If you don't know a competent lawyer whom you would trust to handle your affairs, make it your business to interview several and choose one you feel comfortable with. When a legal problem occurs—and sooner or later, it will—

you will have a good attorney who knows you and what your business is about.

Like doctors, lawyers tend to specialize. Just as you wouldn't go to an ophthalmologist for brain surgery, you don't go to an estate-planning attorney if you're being sued for product liability or if you're suing a party for collection. A good attorney will tell you if he can't handle your problem and will refer you to one who can.

You may find it worthwhile to run your home-based-business idea by an attorney to make sure it's in compliance with local zoning regulations. And it's an excellent idea to have your attorney examine all business transactions involving property or large sums of money. Better to be safe than sorry. But don't wait until an urgent problem strikes and you're in the panic mode to find a good lawyer. Do it while it's important and not urgent.

Financial Planners: Gold Mines and Land Mines

This final member of your professional advisory team can be your greatest ally or your worst nemesis. This is the person you entrust to counsel you on where to invest the money you accumulate to grow your nest egg into your first million.

Of course, it isn't imperative to have a financial planner, and many people in retrospect wish they hadn't had one. You can just shovel the money into bank certificates of deposit, but taxes and inflation will slowly erode its purchasing power over time. And if you have the time and inclination, you can study up on investments and make them from home via your computer or telephone. That may be the least-cost alternative. But think about the time it's taking away from your business, time that you could be using to bring in more money. So for many of us, it's a good idea to pay someone to plan, invest, and manage our money while we concentrate on doing what we do best.

The problem with the financial-planning profession is that

it's very loosely regulated and filled with snake-oil salesmen. This is an area where you can't be too careful, because the wrong financial adviser can wipe you out. Beware of slick operators calling themselves financial planners who want to sell you can't-miss opportunities. Once again, if it sounds too good to be true, it probably is.

The best route is to find a good financial planner and pay him a fee to lay out a long-range financial plan for you. He will ask you about your current income, net worth, and what your financial goals are. Then he will create a plan to get you from where you are to where you want to go. And he will recommend that your portfolio be diversified into a variety of investments, such as stocks, bonds, mutual funds, and government securities.

You can obtain a list of financial planners in your area from trade associations such as the Institute of Certified Financial Planners in Denver (800-282-7526). But having their names on a list only proves they have taken a number of courses. It won't tell you anything about their honesty and integrity. The best source is someone in a financial situation similar to yours who has been using the same planner at least five years and is happy with the work he has done.

Interview several planners and check them out thoroughly. How are they compensated? Some charge nothing for planning and are paid a commission on the products they sell to you. Their main incentive isn't to look out for your financial well-being but to sell you what makes them the most money. Others will charge you a fee to set up a plan and a fee of one to three percent to manage your account. That's better, because as your portfolio grows, so does their money-management fee. Most planners work on some combination of fees plus commissions. Just make sure the incentive is structured so that they get richer for making you richer and not for selling you the latest hot investment product.

A financial planner who is managing your money will provide you with a quarterly itemized statement listing the current value of your investments and the net increase or decrease of your portfolio for the quarter. Insist on this and on the right to cancel his services at any time.

PARTNERING WITH CUSTOMERS, SUPPLIERS, AND OTHERS

In case you haven't noticed, there's a revolution going on in the way businesses of all sizes are relating to each other. Simply put, buyers and sellers are getting married, and businesses are forming alliances. Large companies are reducing their number of suppliers and demanding lower prices. In return, the suppliers get long-term customers and more business. Businesses of all sizes realize that it's much more profitable to treat customers like lifetime partners. And both large and small businesses are teaming up to find new ways for all parties to get richer.

What's new about all this? Plenty. In the old days, buying from suppliers and selling to customers was more adversarial. The primary purpose was to buy from suppliers at the cheapest possible price and sell to customers at the highest possible price. There was little concern if the supplier went under or the customer paid top dollar. And forming alliances with other businesses was far less common. Business was war, the pie was assumed to be fixed, and the goal of every business was to get the biggest piece of the pie.

Fortunately, the pace of change has forced us to rethink the way we do business. Instead of fighting for a bigger piece of the pie, we have come to realize that it's much more profitable to work together and create a bigger pie.

Treat Your Customers Like Lifetime Partners

Treating your customers like partners is one of the best things you can do for your business and your customers. A lifetime partner isn't someone you manipulate into buying what you happen to be selling. He's someone you listen to so you can help him get what he wants by doing business with you. He isn't someone whose problems and special requests are treated lightly. You want him to know that *nobody* is going to take better care of him than you will. Once the customer knows this, he won't even consider taking his business anywhere else. You become his friend, someone he knows he can depend on, and buying from you becomes a habit. Best of all, by referring new customers to you, he acts as your advertising agency and goodwill ambassador rolled into one. Not bad, when you consider that he's paying you. Even if you never see the customer again, treating him that way will still be profitable. You're building a great reputation, and nothing builds a business better or faster than a great reputation.

Treat Your Suppliers as Well as You Treat Your Customers

You may be thinking, To my suppliers, I'm the customer. Why should I treat them as so special? Here's my answer: *Because you need them.* Reciprocity is the basis of all good relationships. The better you treat them, the better they will treat you.

Cash-management experts contend that you should hold off paying suppliers until the latest possible date. You may earn a few extra dollars in interest by keeping the money in your account, but from a partnership standpoint it's shortsighted. Who wants to work closely with people who are going to hold out on them? Pay your bills as soon as you get them, and you'll be much more appreciated.

Give as much of your business to as few suppliers as you can. You'll be a more important customer and will likely get better treatment and better prices. And finally, just as it's wise to get customer feedback, you need to get supplier feedback. Sit down with each of your suppliers and see if you can come up with some answers to questions such as:

- How can we work together to make our relationship more mutually profitable?

- What information do you need to make my business easier to work with?
- What do I need to know about your business so we can better coordinate activities?
- Am I doing anything that makes it difficult for you to work with me?
- What can I do to help you get orders to me faster?
- What can we do to create more value for the consumer?

It's important to remember that the success of both your and your supplier's business depends on pleasing that final link in the "food chain" of business—the customer. Once you are aware of that basic fact, the need to treat your suppliers as well as you treat your customers becomes apparent.

Synergize Your Business Through Alliances

Another important key to growing your business is to form alliances with other businesses to achieve benefits that neither can achieve working alone. Here are some suggestions that you may find potentially profitable:

- Band together with other micropreneurs to buy products in large quantities. Office supplies, computers, and other office equipment can be purchased in quantities at a lower cost per unit.

- Pool your marketing efforts with complementary businesses. For example, a bridal consultant might create a brochure with a caterer, photographer, and reception hall. All businesses get the benefits of marketing, and the cost of the brochure is split four ways.

- Barter your products or services with other businesses, which is less costly and more profitable for both of you.

• Instead of hiring employees, outsource jobs to other micropreneurs or larger businesses. Everything from clerical chores to sales can be outsourced.

• Form a mastermind group of micropreneurs whose purpose is to provide information, encouragement, and support for all its members. Whenever someone in the group has a problem, chances are that someone else has had a similar one and solved it. Instead of reinventing the wheel, you can learn and profit from each other's experiences. If the group needs information, you can hire a business consultant to work with the group. Or you can buy books and cassette tapes, pass them around, and split the cost.

• Participate in a joint venture with other micropreneurs that capitalizes on the strengths of all parties. For example, I know three people who successfully put on a profitable public seminar. One supplied the capital, one marketed the seminar, and the third party produced and presented it.

When you and other parties form an alliance that involves sharing costs or splitting revenues, put the agreement in writing and have all parties read and sign it. This can prevent a lot of potential future headaches and conflicts. It's also a good idea to have an agreement in writing about who is responsible for doing what and about the procedures to be followed when the alliance is dissolved or one or more parties wants to leave. For example, it might be wise to have all partners sign a noncompetition clause in the event that they leave the alliance.

When you decide to form alliances, it's always tempting to look for friends or relatives to work with. You know, like, and trust them. But keep in mind that working with people and socializing with them are two entirely different things. I've seen some successful business ventures created by friends, and I've seen many wonderful, long-lasting relationships ruined over business deals. Before deciding to work with friends, you may want to heed the words of John D. Rockefeller: "A friendship built on business is better than a business built on friendship."

Today's big corporations are downsizing, outsourcing, and forming alliances more than ever. Their purpose is to reduce fixed costs and gain the freedom and flexibility to focus on their most profitable activities. And that's precisely what good partners can do to help turn a home-based micropreneur into a homemade millionaire. As an Ethiopian proverb states, "When spider webs unite, they can tie up a lion."

Resolve Problems and Conflicts the Win/Win Way

Inasmuch as people aren't perfect, neither are relationships. Conflicts and problems with partners will inevitably arise. The key to successfully resolving any type of conflict is to realize that how you go about resolving it is far more important than the problem itself.

The instinctive approach to settling a conflict is to dig in your heels and think either/or: Either they get what they want, or you get what you want. That approach usually results in wars, divorces, lawsuits, hurt feelings, lost customers, and the end of successful business relationships. A far better approach is win/win—working with the other party to find a solution that benefits everyone. It takes time and effort, but it's far less costly and far more profitable in the long run. Here are some guidelines to help you resolve problems and conflicts constructively:

1. Decide what you want. Whether it's to satisfy an angry customer, get a better price from a supplier, or improve the performance of an ally, you need to focus on the goal you're trying to achieve that's being blocked by the conflict.

2. Back off and separate yourself emotionally from the problem. Think of yourself as a third party observing two

other people and don't allow your emotions to be drawn into the picture. Letting your emotions take over decreases your ability to think clearly and increases the odds of more frustration.

3. Do your homework. Find out what the other party wants. Conflict arises because people have differing points of view and different interests. Put yourself in their shoes. What are their interests? What are they trying to achieve? Ask yourself, If I were they, how would I feel about the situation? The best way to find out is to ask them.

4. Attack the problem and not the person. You don't want to make him angry or put him on the defensive because that will just shut down the communication necessary to resolve the conflict. Communicate with the other person in a relaxed, nonjudgmental way. Speak in a calm tone of voice. Don't interrupt or contradict him. Remove physical barriers; for example, don't sit behind a desk. And don't speak in terms of either/or solutions.

5. Once you learn what he wants, explain what you want and say, "Let's see if we can come up with some new options that will be good for both of us." Then brainstorm some new ideas. Don't judge the new ideas. Just write them down. There are an infinite number of ideas in the universe, and at least several of them will work if both of you want to solve the problem.

6. Once you arrive at a satisfactory solution, agree on it and put it into action. Don't expect to get everything that you want. You want to preserve the relationship and have the other party leave the table feeling that he got a good deal, too. Once again, if it involves something substantial, you may want to put the final agreement in writing.

If you can't resolve the conflict, don't get angry or leave the other party with a bad impression of you. Just say, "I'm sorry we couldn't work this out," walk away politely, and move on. One of the great laws of life is that friends come and go, but enemies accumulate. If you're a micropreneur, you can't have too many people saying nice things about you and too few people saying bad things about you.

WARNING: READ THIS BEFORE HIRING SOMEONE

Let's assume you're a successful micropreneur. Your sales are growing and your customers are coming back. You're making more money than you ever imagined, and you have more business than you can handle. You think to yourself, If only I had someone to help me, my work and my life would be so much easier, and I could bring in more money. STOP!

Deciding to add an employee to your business changes everything. While it may be profitable, it will also take your business to a new level of complexity and give it a whole new set of problems and headaches. For example:

• In addition to being a business owner, you're now a manager, and your freedom and flexibility will be forever restricted. To restrict your freedom is to defeat the biggest benefit of being a micropreneur. Instead of running a business, you run the risk of the business running you.

• If you want the employee to work in your office, you have to provide space and equipment for him or her. Assuming it's not a member of your family, you give up your privacy if an outsider comes to work in your home.

• You're now responsible for bringing in enough additional revenue to cover an employee's salary plus all the fringe benefits you may need to provide, such as health care and pension plans.

• Our friends in the government will add to your administrative burdens by requiring you to withhold an employee's taxes and Social Security payments, and will require of you a host of other record-keeping chores.

• You have to train employees and endure their mistakes for a period of time before they are earning their keep. And every time someone quits, you have to start all over.

• If you're depending on employees and they don't show up for work, you have change your plans and do their work, too, or the work doesn't get done.

• When your employees make a mistake or anger a customer, you're responsible for righting the wrongs.

• The more time you need to devote to managing, the less time you have to do what you need to do to bring in the money.

• In short, by hiring employees, you run a high risk of lowering your profits. Having more employees doesn't always mean higher profits but it always means higher overhead. And low overhead is the secret to a successful home-based business.

Of course, you aren't going to become the next General Motors or Microsoft without staff. And there are times when you will need extra hands, such as when you're sick, have pressing family responsibilities, or have more business than you can handle. Fortunately, there are other options for such times.

One option is to ally yourself with another micropreneur in your type of business and agree to serve as a backup for each other. Whenever it's impossible for you to fulfill a commitment to a customer, your backup will provide the product or service. If you have such an arrangement, be sure to agree in advance how each of you will be compensated.

Another option is to hire temporary employees on a contractual basis for a specified period of time. Like home-based businesses, temporary employment is the wave of the present and future. The temporary-employment sector grew ten times faster than overall employment during the decade of the eighties. Today the number of freelancers, contractors, leased employees, and part-timers is over 37 million strong in the United States and growing. Manpower Inc., a temporary-employment agency, is the largest private employer in the United States.

If you're thinking about hiring an employee, sure, it would be nice to have someone to answer the phone, run errands, make photocopies, and type letters. But with technology getting more capable and cheaper every day, the rationale for hiring makes less sense. Remember, what you don't start, you don't have to finish. And by choosing and working successfully with partners, you can create a great staff without ever hiring a single full-time employee. Comedian Tim Allen put it best when he wrote, "All men like to think they can do it alone, but a real man knows that there's no substitute for support, encouragement, and a pit crew."

12

How to Be Your Own Best Boss

Always bear in mind that your own resolution to succeed is more important than any one thing.

—ABRAHAM LINCOLN

Everybody needs a very special mentor, and you're no exception. You need someone to convince you that you're better than you think you are. You need someone who will make you develop the skills that are required for exceptional success. You need someone to guide you, encourage you, and point the way to heights you've never dreamed of. You need someone who will pick you up when you fall down and restore your spirit and determination after disappointing setbacks. In short, to be a homemade millionaire, you need a personal motivator, teacher, coach, and best friend who will stand by you no matter what the future brings.

Well, guess what? I've got the perfect person for you. Go look in the mirror. You need *you.*

Your journey to success starts on the day you realize that no one else is going to make it for you. We all need partners. We all want the encouragement and support of others. Get all you can and reciprocate whenever possible. But have the courage to face a most obvious truth about your own success:

IT'S UP TO YOU. Ty Boyd, my friend and a consummate professional speaker, put it best when he said:

> *What I have learned is . . . there ain't no genie. I am it. If the*
> *wealth and adventure and fame are to come, I'd better get tough*
> *on the only one who can make it happen . . . me!*

It's been said that every person is self-made but only the successful are willing to admit it. When you're on your own, no one is going to impose discipline on you. No one tells you when to work, when to take a break, or when to end the workday. No one gives you a raise or a two-week vacation with pay. No one gives you a kick in the pants or a pat on the back when you need it. In short, there's no direction, no structure, no motivation, and no consistent effort unless *you* provide it. You have to master the arts of self-discipline, patience, and persistence because without a healthy amount of each, your chances of success are slim to none.

THE BASICS OF BEING YOUR OWN BEST BOSS

When he was at the peak of his career, Henry Fonda was asked what he considered the most important thing a young actor could learn. Fonda replied, "How to become an old actor." We all know ambitious, talented, hardworking people who fail to achieve meaningful success. Why? One key reason is that they concentrate solely on mastering their work, while the important job of mastering themselves goes neglected. With that thought in mind, here are six basic self-management strategies to help you have a long, successful, enjoyable career as a micropreneur.

1. Creating Wealth Requires Good Health.

An old joke has it that one businessman said to another, "Money isn't everything. Health is three percent." Rule number one for being your own best boss is to realize that your health is job number one. The business world is filled with people who sacrifice their health to make a fortune and then spend what they earned trying to buy it back. Don't be one of them. Lose your health and you lose much, if not all, of your earning capacity. More important, even if you make a fortune, you won't be able to enjoy it. Nothing, absolutely nothing, is more important than maintaining and improving your physical and mental well-being. If you have your health, you're wealthy. The rest is icing on the cake.

If you smoke, quit. If you drink, do it in moderation. Watch your weight. Eat healthy foods. And get enough rest to put in a good day's work.

I strongly believe that people who don't invest the time to stay healthy must eventually make the time to be sick. If you don't exercise regularly, start doing it for at least half an hour every other day. Join a health club. Ride a bicycle. Swim. Walk briskly. To combat boredom, work out with a friend or listen to tapes or the radio. Put an exercise bike in front of your TV and use it. Your choice of exercise isn't important. Just do something that you enjoy and that gets your heart rate up for at least 20 minutes. Check with your doctor before beginning and read a good book on physical fitness. Once you get in the exercise habit, you'll get hooked on it because you'll realize how much better you look and feel. Invest the time to become physically fit and you'll earn more.

2. Lead a Balanced Life.

It's easy to be consumed by your work when you run your own show. You're doing what you want to do, and you have an intense desire to succeed. But like ignoring your health, ignoring other aspects of your life can be very shortsighted and destructive to both your business and personal life. It's hard to concentrate on your work when your personal life is going poorly.

Contrary to what they would like you to think, workaholics

aren't the most productive people. Because they work long hours, they tend to develop inefficient work habits and get bogged down in trivia. To the workaholic, work becomes an end in itself. The most productive and successful people live for their work and a whole lot more.

Make it your business to set aside plenty of time for non-work activities. Take two days a week off. Spend that hour a day you used to spend commuting to work with your spouse, your children, or your friends, or on a new hobby. Make it your business to take at least a few weeks off every year. You'll come back rested with a fresh perspective and a host of new ideas for growing your business. It's like being in good health; you'll find that when the rest of your life is in balance your earning capacity increases.

Naturally, there will be periods of time when you have to put in long hours to do what needs to be done, especially in the beginning. We all pay the price for success in one way or another. The important thing is to keep your work in perspective and not get tired of it. Creating and running the perfect business isn't an end in itself. It's only a means to a better life.

3. Stay Focused.

Remember that you'll become what you think about most of the time. So make it a habit to think regularly and often about your long-term purpose. Read your mission and vision statements, The Most Important Question, and your Most Important Goals list at least once each workday. That's the first step to staying focused.

The next step is to do something every working day that moves you closer to the long-term results you want to achieve. You want to become a millionaire? What can you do today that will move you a step closer to that goal? It doesn't have to be a giant step. You just have to keep moving toward your ultimate target each day. As in golf, you don't have to hit the ball fast or far. You just have to hit it straight. A major key to success lies in knowing the difference between motion and direction.

Psychologists discovered long ago that people tend to stay focused on work, play, or any activity if the activity has four key ingredients:

- A goal.
- A way to keep score.
- Control over the situation.
- Rewards for achieving the goal.

As your own boss, your job is to provide those four ingredients for yourself. Choose the results you want to achieve and the way you're going to measure and track your progress. You're already in control of the situation. And if you answered The Most Important Question, you already know what rewards are in it for you. Whatever your business, if it has those four ingredients, you'll stay focused.

4. Don't Compete with Anyone but Yourself.

I'm a great believer in free enterprise and the spirit of competition. It creates wealth and results in the best products and services at the lowest prices. But having said that, I also think that it's a mistake to compete directly with and compare yourself to others. Don't compete, create. Nobody in the entire history of the world has your unique combination of brains, talent, knowledge, and experience. Capitalize on your unique set of strengths to create something that people are willing to pay for. To do what others are doing in the exact same way and directly compete with them is just another way of playing follow-the-leader. As my friend, author Sheila Murray Bethel, says, "Managers have 'to do' lists. Leaders have 'to create' lists."

You can and should learn what the best people in your industry do and how they do it. Many businesses benefit from "benchmarking"—using as a standard the best business practices of excellent companies. That's great, and I would encourage you to learn from the best people in your field. But it's a mistake to think that you can be just like or better than they are. It's like comparing apples with oranges.

Comparing yourself or your achievements with others is a counterproductive waste of time. The only person you should directly compete with is the person you were yesterday. If you're getting better every day, someday you're going to be among the best, and the money and freedom will come with it.

5. Be a Champion and Not a Victim of Change.

Change is initially difficult for all of us, and we have a natural tendency to resist it. Yet, like it or not, we live in an era of unprecedented, rapid, accelerating change. As my friend Dan Burrus wrote in his book, *Technotrends,* "If it works, it's obsolete."

What's important to realize about change is that you have a choice. You can resist it and become a victim, or you can choose to be a champion of change and capitalize on it. The technology that's eliminating jobs in the corporate world is the same technology that's making it possible to make a million from home.

The surest way to become a victim of change is to ignore it. Just bury your head in the sand, keep doing things the same old way you've always done them, and the world will soon pass you by. There's an enormous temptation to do this, especially when we enjoy success. But it's important to realize that it is when we are successful that we are also the most vulnerable. Once again, if it works, it's obsolete.

To become a champion of change requires having the courage to get out of your comfort zone and try new things before you are forced to. All change involves risk. That's why we resist it. But it's through the process of change that you grow and improve both as a micropreneur and as a person.

Make it a habit always to pursue some innovative goals. To

set innovative goals, begin by answering this question: *What can I do that I'm not doing now that would make my business more profitable?* Can you create new products and services? Can you find new ways to market the ones you currently have? What new smart tools can you learn how to use to make your operation more productive? What new skills can you learn or improve on that will grow your business? What new people can you meet who might provide new business opportunities for you? Recognizing the need for change is essential. And becoming a champion of change is a necessity for growth. The big winners in any type of business are the ones who understand how the world is changing and adapt accordingly.

6. Sidestep the Special Problems of Working from Home.

If you work in a nine-to-five job with a long commute, the prospect of being a home-based micropreneur probably sounds incredibly wonderful. You don't have to be at work at a certain time, you don't have to wear a coat and tie or high heels to work, and you can call it a day whenever you feel like it. It may even sound too good to be true.

Let me assure you that it *is* wonderful. After having been my own boss, the thought of getting up every day and going to work for someone else seems terribly unpleasant. But being your own home-based boss, like everything else, has its own set of problems.

One of the new problems you're likely to encounter is a sense of isolation and loneliness. After years of working in an office, teaching students, or calling on customers, you're suddenly all by yourself for hours every day. Unless you're a total recluse, this can be a very daunting prospect. We all need people-contact. So make it a habit to get out of the house at least once and preferably twice a day. Meet friends for lunch or dinner. Join a volunteer organization or home-based-business group of other micropreneurs. Exercise with a friend. Stay in touch with friends via the telephone, fax, or computer. Working alone doesn't mean you have to be lonely. You just have to make a conscious effort to get out and see people as often as you feel the need.

A second problem is separating your work life from the rest of your life. As wonderful and interesting as your work may be, you need to turn it off when the workday is over. Otherwise, you'll burn out. Have a separate space, preferably an entire room, that's reserved for work. If you don't have room for an office, put up a screen or some kind of partition around your work area. Have a separate phone line for your business. When your work is done, you want to be able to close the door on it so you can turn your attention to being a good spouse, parent, neighbor, sports fan, hobbyist, friend, or whatever. The worst example of a home office setup that I can think of is a card table in the corner of your bedroom.

A third problem that you're likely to confront is resisting all the temptations, interruptions, and distractions that can keep you from working. Watching television, visiting or calling friends, being interrupted by family members, and raiding the refrigerator are all welcome distractions that keep you from doing what you need to do. The way to overcome them is simply to treat your home-based business like a job. Establish a separate place and specific hours so you can work undisturbed. No television. No personal phone calls. No food, except for breaks. No domestic interruptions unless there's an emergency.

Decide at the start of every workday what you want to get done, write it down, and do it. Some people find it helpful to dress a certain way as a cue to themselves that it's time to go to work. Do only work-related tasks in your office, and that will be another cue that it's time to go to work when you step in your office. Working from home is not a perennial vacation. Making a million doesn't come from the hours you put in your work, but from the work you put in your hours.

A final problem you may confront is convincing friends, neighbors, and family members that working from home is WORK. You aren't on tap for drop-in visits, watching their children, running errands, or listening to their problems during work hours. Politely tell others, "This is my new job. If I don't make a go of it, I'm going to have to get another job or ask you to support me." They wouldn't dream of making such demands of you if you worked in a traditional office setting unless there was a dire emergency. Explain that the rules haven't changed, just the nature and location of your work. Get a Do Not Disturb sign and hang it on your office door or front door during work hours. If the doorbell or the family telephone rings, there's no law that says you have to answer it.

PATIENCE AND PERSISTENCE ARE OMNIPOTENT

Over the years I've come to realize a very important truth about life. *With enough patience and persistence, you can have just about anything you want.* You can't have *everything* you want, and that's probably a good thing. If you had it all, what would you do with it? Remember, what you own, owns you!

Most people don't achieve their dreams because they haven't taken the time to decide what they really want and focus their time and energy on achieving it. But let's assume you're different. You've decided you want to be a homemade millionaire, and you've picked a business that's right for you and is capable of making a million for you in due time. If that's true, all you need now is to go to work each day pursuing your goals and living your vision, and you'll get there. When? I can't tell you that because each person and each business is different. But if you work, save, invest, and continue to enjoy reasonably good health, you *will* get there. And someday, many years from now, you'll look back on it all and realize that you have achieved a level of success far beyond your wildest expectations. But that's for tomorrow.

The task in front of you today and for the immediate future is to plan your work and work your plan. Easier said than done? You bet. But with desire, focus, and intelligent persistence, I'll say it again, you *will* get there. The key is staying motivated to work and committed to your course of action.

To be sure, talent, knowledge, knowing the right people, and luck will play a part. But the one thing all successful people have in common is plain old tenacity. As Winston Churchill remarked, "If there is no wind, row."

The Gods Will Test You

Trust me on this: No matter how talented, how ambitious, or how initially lucky you are, there are going to be disappointments, setbacks, and days when you just want to chuck it all— particularly in the beginning. When that happens, simply realize that you're being tested. If you give in, you fail. If you persist, you pass. And if you persist long enough, you become a homemade millionaire. The choice is yours. Keep the faith, do the work, and you'll get the fortune.

Like everything else in life, the long-range impact of tough times will not be determined by what happens to you but what you *think* about what happens to you and what you *choose* to do about it. Once you understand and accept the fact that you're in control of your mind and your destiny, you can use any experience as a valuable lesson in learning. Here are some things to do and points to keep in mind when adversity strikes:

1. Remember that success teaches you nothing. Buried in the setbacks and hard times are the seeds of future victories, if we're smart enough to look for them. When misfortune strikes, ask yourself, What can I learn from this that will enable me to reach my goals? and What will I do differently next time? If it's important, write it down and resolve to use what you've learned next time.

My friend J. T. Curtis is one of the winningest high school football coaches in the nation. In 25 years of coaching, his teams have won 12 state championships. For over a decade, his teams haven't lost a regular season game. Whenever they lose, it's in the state playoffs and not by much. One way Curtis keeps his team sharp is by reviewing game films of victories as if they were defeats. He's smart enough to realize that success breeds complacency. The seeds of future victories can only be found through continuous learning and improvement.

2. Keep a success log. Every life is a combination of victories and setbacks, and yours is no exception. When tough times hit, you need to keep your spirits up. One good way is to remind yourself of the battles you've won. Write down on a sheet of paper the victories of your life—that raise you got, the promotion you won, the first big sale you made in your home-based business, or the complimentary letter you received from a satisfied customer. As you enjoy new successes, celebrate and add them to the log. If you start writing them down, you'll be amazed at the good things that you've made happen in your life. And you'll make even bigger and better ones happen in the future.

3. When you get knocked down, get back up. Learn from misfortune, but don't dwell on it and don't let it immobilize you. Pick yourself up, take a deep breath, and get busy pursuing your goals. One of my favorite definitions of success is "going from failure to failure with great enthusiasm." Successful people are masters at the art of bounce-back-ability.

Get a group of successful entrepreneurs together and you'll hear stories of how many different businesses they tried until they found one that hit big. And many, if not most of them, will tell you that the best thing that ever happened to them was being fired from a job. It was their first step on the road to great wealth.

The champion of bounce-back-ability is my friend W. Mitchell. Perhaps you've read about Mitchell, as his friends call him, or heard him speak. He has been dubbed "The Man Who Will Not Be Defeated," and for good reason. As a young man in 1971, he had the misfortune of being badly burned in a motorcycle accident. With burns over 65 percent of his body, his face and most of his hands were literally burned off. Four years later, he was flying his own airplane when it crashed, leaving him a paraplegic. But if you think misfortune has prevented him from living a wonderful, productive life, you don't know Mitchell. He became a millionaire. He married. He owns property in Hawaii, Colorado, and California. He ran for political office, and is a fantastic motivational speaker and a wonderful human being whose contributions make the world a better place. About his life, Mitchell says, "It isn't what happens to you, it's what you do about it. . . . Before all this happened to me there were ten thousand things I could do. Now there are nine thousand. I could spend my life dwelling on the thousand I lost, but I choose to focus on the nine thousand that are left."

Whenever I'm having a bad day, I think about Mitchell's philosophy, look at myself in the mirror, and say, "What's your problem?" I remind myself that if there weren't bad days, I wouldn't know what a good day was. Then I go back to work.

4. Remember the great cliché, "It takes 15 years to become an overnight success." It's a cliché because it's true. As the opera singer Beverly Sills put it, "There are no shortcuts to any place worth going."

We live in an era of push-button need-gratification. Almost every day the media has stories about young entertainers and sports figures signing multimillion-dollar contracts. The odds of that happening to you are about as good as your chances of winning the lottery. For the majority of us, making a fortune takes years of time, effort, and learning. If you make it in less than 15 years, that's great. Count your blessings. As Arnold H. Glasgow wrote, "The key to everything is patience. You get the chicken by hatching the egg, not by smashing it."

What if you don't want to work, save, and invest for 15 years? That's fine with me. But remember that those years are going to pass no matter what you do. It's your life and you have to live it. The only thing certain is that you'll be 15 years older than you are today. If you're like most people, you'll be living modestly, working for someone else, worrying about paying your bills, and complaining about how other people got all the breaks. Yeah, right.

But if you do decide to become a micropreneur and you keep learning and working, someday you're going to hit . . .

The Critical Mass

You work and work and work, persisting over the years, wondering if you're wasting your time. But you aren't wasting your time. You're learning, investing in yourself, and building momentum. Then one day something wonderful happens, and making money becomes very easy. Suddenly you find yourself making 5, 10, or 20 times as much money as the year before, and you aren't working any harder. In fact, you may be working less. This happens thousands of times every day to people who have had the courage to pursue their dreams and persist. And it will happen to you too.

What to Do Once You've Made It

What a wonderful day it is when you realize that your money problems are over. You have complete freedom to live wherever you want and use your time any way you like. The rest of your life will be the best of your life—if you're smart.

Making a million doesn't prevent you from losing it. Never forget that, and manage your money wisely. But with that as a given, what are you going to do with all that freedom you've earned? If you're like me, you'll continue to work. If you picked the perfect business, you'll still have a passion for it even though you're rich. While you may not want to work as hard and may take more time off, complete idleness is very unfulfilling as well as life shortening. People with a sense of purpose who enjoy what they're doing live happier, healthier, and longer lives.

Start working on your next million. Don't ever retire unless the work becomes unpleasant or you're bored with it. The work you find challenging and enjoyable when you aren't financially independent becomes even more enjoyable when you are. You have the freedom to do as much or as little of it as you like. It's the best of all worlds—a hobby that pays!

Once you're financially set for life, the world is your oyster. You've been promoted to the class of the fortunate few. You're no longer a slave to the alarm clock, dependent on the whims of a boss, or worried about paying your bills. Your former colleagues from work will hear about your good fortune, shake their heads in disbelief, and say, "How lucky can you get?" But you'll know better. You made that luck.

EPILOGUE

The Climb Is Better Than the View

You now have the road map for your journey to becoming a homemade millionaire. If you haven't already started, I hope you'll choose a business that's right for you and begin working toward achieving the wealth and freedom you deserve. But I want to leave you with one more point that may be the most important one of all:

Take time to savor and enjoy each step of the journey.

Once you arrive, you'll realize that the real fun isn't being there. It was getting there. It's the work you do, the people you meet, and the experiences you have along the way that really make the journey worthwhile. So take time every day to smell the roses and savor every experience, even the bad ones—because you're living your life your way. And life doesn't get any better than that.

INDEX

ABOUT THE AUTHOR

Michael LeBoeuf's mission is to help people find solid, practical ways to live and work smarter. He is an internationally published author and business consultant and a dynamic professional speaker and seminar leader. A former university professor, Dr. LeBoeuf received his Ph.D. from Louisiana State University and taught courses in management, organizational behavior, and communication at the University of New Orleans for twenty years, retiring as professor emeritus in 1989.

His previous books, which include *Working Smart, Getting Results* (formerly published as *GMP: The Greatest Management Principle in the World*), and *How to Win Customers and Keep Them for Life,* have been published in over a dozen different languages, selected by major book clubs, and excerpted in newspapers and magazines on all continents. In addition, his books have been adapted to produce 13 best-selling audio-cassette and video-based training programs.

In constant demand as a speaker, Dr. LeBoeuf addresses business and professional audiences worldwide. He has appeared on hundreds of radio and television shows, including *Good Morning America* and the *CBS Evening News.* As both a speaker and a writer, his ability to communicate with clarity and enthusiasm makes him a popular favorite. He lives in Scottsdale, Arizona.